PICTORIAL HISTORY
OF THE ROYAL NAVY

By the same author

THE LOSS OF THE SCHARNHORST
JAPANESE WARSHIPS OF WORLD WAR II
THE IMPERIAL JAPANESE NAVY 1865-1945
(in preparation)

PICTORIAL HISTORY
OF THE
Royal Navy

ANTHONY J. WATTS

VOLUME ONE · 1816–1880

LONDON

IAN ALLAN

First published 1970

SBN 7110 0186 3

*Published by Ian Allan Ltd, Shepperton, Surrey and printed in
Great Britain by Morrison and Gibb Ltd, London and Edinburgh*

Contents

Foreword

THE ROYAL NAVY of today is a small, highly compact and efficient force, the ships being highly complex technological weapons, manned more by a special breed of scientists than by ordinary men. No longer are naval reviews held, when line upon line of battleships stretch across the Solent as far as the eye can see. Each passing year sees more ships sent to the scrap-heap, with fewer replacements from the shipyards. Each year the commitments are reduced as the British pull out from yet another overseas base or colony. Still, however, the navy is needed. Great Britain is an island and the navy has paramount importance in ensuring that the sea lanes are kept open and the imports, so vital to the life of this country, keep rolling in.

In this *Pictorial History of the Royal Navy* the evolution of the navy from 1816 to 1870 is described. During this period the conditions of service for seamen underwent revolutionary changes, as did the ships themselves. By the end of 1870 most of the major technological advances had been achieved, and the line of development for the next fifty years had been set. With these changes complete the service was placed firmly on its feet.

In a concise volume of this nature it is not possible to include all developments concerned with the history and evolution during the changeover from sail to steam.

I should like to acknowledge my thanks for all the help extended to me by many people and especially to Miss L. Boutroy of the Mansell Collection and to Miss Shepherd of the Radio Times Hulton Picture Library and also to the staff of the photographic departments of the National Maritime Museum and the Imperial War Museum. Finally I should like to thank my wife for all the help and encouragement she has given me during my research for this work.

Introduction

EVER SINCE Sir Francis Drake chased the Spanish Armada up the English Channel to its destruction around the coasts of Great Britain, and Queen Elizabeth the First refused to be intimidated by Philip of Spain, two matters have always exercised the mind of the man in the street in Great Britain. They are the Royal Navy and the National Policy of the British Government. For hundreds of years the two have gone hand in hand, each more or less dependent on the other.

The dawn of the nineteenth century heralded vast changes, both for Great Britain as a nation and for the Royal Navy as a force designed to keep the island on the map. The great period of the Napoleonic Wars ended in 1815 when Napoleon Bonaparte surrendered his Emperor's crown on board the *Bellerophon* and was taken on his last journey to exile on the lonely island of St. Helena, where he eventually died in 1821.

With the banishment of Napoleon peace fell over Europe, a peace ensured by the ever-growing presence of the Royal Navy, of whom Napoleon once said, "Wherever there is water to float a ship, we are sure to find you in the way". This was to be the dawn of the great peace; peace for Great Britain and also for a large part of the world. The period of the "Pax Britannica" might also have been called the "Golden Age of Colonialism". Not only did Great Britain expand to become the largest Empire in the world under the austere personage of Queen Victoria (1837 to 1901), but other countries also extended their spheres of influence. Under the expert guidance of Chancellor Bismarck the multitude of German States unified in 1871 and slowly began to build the Kaiser's Empire in Africa and the Far East. Italy was also unified in 1860 together with some unofficial and official assistance from the Royal Navy. One other Empire which must be mentioned in this age of expansion—the Japanese—was usually ignored by most of the Western Hemisphere. After unification in 1868 Japan expanded to such an extent, with such powerful forces, that it clearly rivalled the other great Empires in the world. Japan held almost complete sway in the Far East (except India) and continued to consolidate her gains, completely overshadowing the Chinese and Russian Empires, and upsetting the balance of power in that part of the world.

Apart from these expanding Empires one continent made up of many states and tribes was rapidly coming into the limelight—Africa. Great

9

Britain and Germany were already busy staking out their claims and colonising large parts of the continent, and were closely followed by the Spanish, Dutch, Portuguese, Belgian and French. Large numbers of settlers and traders were opening up the continent accompanied by the missionaries, and with such riches ready for the plucking it was only natural that there should be conflicts of interest between the states involved in the exploitation of the "Dark Continent". This of course led to many minor incidents, but only one of these developed into a full-scale war—the Boer War.

There were, however, a number of Empires that were slowly on the wane. Amongst these was the Austro-Hungarian Empire which remained under the rule of the Hapsburgs, much as it had done for the previous hundred years or so. The Balkan States, over whom the Emperor—Franz Joseph—held a somewhat tottery rule, continually seethed with discontent. The small states making up the Empire were continually bickering over their boundaries, and the Slavs as a race certainly had no love of the Austrians.

Apart from the Austro-Hungarian Empire in its rather unsteady state of equilibrium, three other large and powerful Empires were clearly beginning to show the signs of decline. The Chinese Empire was split by different factions and in such a disunified state that the expanding Japanese Empire found it easy to appropriate large parts of it such as Korea and Manchuria. The Ottoman Empire was having its troubles too with its Slav areas continually in revolt and Greece seething with anarchy. Although on the surface all appeared calm and serene, serious trouble was also brewing for the Russian Czar, with many secret societies continually plotting his overthrow and the poor peasants almost in bondage.

In this strange state of peace the Royal Navy was preparing to carry out its new tasks. Instead of being engaged in capturing and destroying the merchant shipping of foreign nations its new duties were the protection of those self-same merchantmen.

CHAPTER I

Life in the Navy of 1815

May humanity after victory be the predominant feature in the British Fleet

NELSON

WITH THE ENDING in 1815 of the Napoleonic Wars the British Government began gradually to change certain of its policies and, as a result, the role of the Royal Navy underwent an almost imperceptible change. The previous two centuries had seen the British busily engaged in expanding their trading interests overseas. As Napoleon once said, we were "a nation of shopkeepers", trading all over the world. In order to expand this trade we could not afford to have competitors and this gave rise to numerous wars in which the Royal Navy played the greater role, protecting our own trading interests and attacking the vessels of any nation who interfered with the free passage of our own merchant ships.

As an instrument of national policy the navy was responsible for ensuring the freedom of the seas for British shipping and its warships had been organised for this role. To pursue a policy of mercantile trade (trade restricted to selling only) the navy was called upon to engage the forces of France, Holland, Portugal and Spain in order that Great Britain might gain the monopoly of any trade.

After 1815 this policy began to change. Great Britain had the monopoly of trade and at that time her navy was the strongest in the world and her merchant fleet the largest. Thus situated the British Government decided that their interests could best be served by a policy of free trade as opposed to mercantile trade. Instead of fighting to gain a monopoly of trade the Government could afford to be at peace and trade with everyone—the Pax Britannica. With Great Britain leading the world in trade and wealth, it was more profitable for many of her former enemies to trade with her than to fight her and so the role of the Royal Navy changed from that of fighting to that of protecting merchant ships engaged in this free trade. A trade which was gradually extended throughout the world. From giving Great Britain control of the seas the strength of the Royal Navy now ensured that the freedom of the seas was available to all who were engaged in legitimate trading. Woe betide those, however, who sought to prevent others from using the freedom of the seas, or engaged in illicit trading enterprises.

Thus, gradually did the role of the Royal Navy change. Not only the role was to change during the coming years, but the ships too, and even the men themselves. Before long a new kind of sailor would be seen walking the decks of a man-of-war. The changes were to be so dramatic in fact that by the time the nineteenth century ended the only remaining vestige of the old navy would be its tradition. The strict adherence to tradition, however, held with it many disadvantages.

What was the state of the Royal Navy in 1815? As already stated it was the most powerful navy in the world with undisputed command of the seas. In the ships though the men were living and working under much the same conditions as had prevailed at the beginning of the eighteenth century. The ships themselves had not progressed very much either—they were slightly larger and carried more guns, but were still of the same basic design, relying on sail for movement. Conditions for the men on board were abominable, the crews being packed like sardines in the steaming, humid conditions that prevailed below.

The press-gang was still the only real method of making up a ship's complement. As soon as a ship was due to commission notices were posted in various public places in its home port, but there were never enough volunteers, and the press-gang was relied upon to fill up the numerous gaps in the crew list. The first targets for the press-gangs were merchant vessels returning home after long voyages from abroad, thereafter the waterfronts where many seafaring man could be found then lastly the town centres for the landlubbers. Anyone showing any resistance was usually clubbed over the head and carried aboard senseless. It was no use beating the man too hard, however, or he would not be fit for duty the next morning. The real beatings were yet to come for the newly pressed seaman. As a means of recruitment though, the press-gang was reaching the end of its days. On board the vessels of the Royal Navy the "Cat" was king and the captain "God", and the discipline was probably the harshest of any sea-faring nation. "If we do not use the 'cat' the crew will mutiny," was a cry heard from many an admiral and captain. Usually it was because of the cat and such like cruel punishments that the men mutinied.

The harsh discipline and frequent use of the "cat" (the normal punishment being from three to six dozen strokes) together with other equally brutal punishments led to many a man being driven insane. Not only the floggings, though, sent men mad but also the continual knocks and bangs received from the heavy equipment and the large quantities of neat rum that was consumed to drown one's sorrows or pain! (rum being about the only liquid fit to drink on board, each man receiving half a pint a day). In fact it was estimated that in 1815 the Royal Navy had one man in under a thousand insane, whereas in the country as a whole the figure was only one in seven thousand. Such large numbers of seamen were being discharged as insane that the navy had to build its own asylum—the Bethlehem Royal Hospital (Bedlam) —in Moorfields.

Apart from being driven mad many men in the navy were physically disabled as well. The 32-pdr carronade for instance weighted 55cwt and had to be manhandled as did the heavy water casks; lifting tackle was never used. No small wonder then that the men got ruptured. Disablement was also caused in the handling of the heavy canvas sails. With wet weather these became doubly heavy and the men would lie out on the yards using both hands to haul in the sail and handle the ropes, at anything up to 120 feet above the deck, with the vessel often rolling in between 20 and 30 degrees in heavy seas. By 1815 so many men had ruptures and there were so few really fit men ashore—most able bodied men having been conscripted for the Napoleonic Wars—that the Royal Navy was forced to start issuing trusses. The navy's great surgeon, Sir Gilbert Blane, issued on an average 3714 trusses between 1808 and 1815 and estimated that at least one in ten and maybe even one in seven men had ruptures in the Royal Navy.

Between them ruptures and insanity were the two greatest

occupational hazards suffered by men in the navy at this time. There were other hazards of course, diseases such as tuberculosis and the age old scurvy being the commonest. In the cramped and steaming mess decks with 100 sweating men and dripping bulkheads, conditions were ideal for the spread of the disease.

Apart from the occupational hazards suffered by the ordinary seaman, officers also had problems. Theirs, however, was one of promotion. For the ordinary seaman peace in 1815 was a blessed relief, but for many young officers it spelt disaster. Officers were nearly always drawn from the upper class families and were usually found a commission by their parents or a friend of the family with a fairly high commission in the navy. The position of authority for the young man was then assured. For many of these young officers the wars of the eighteenth century were a godsend. Not being entitled to inherit their family fortunes or titles because they were often younger sons, they relied on the prize money awarded from the capture of enemy ships to amass their personal fortune, and often to purchase a title for themselves. The system of promotion was archaic in the extreme. In the early years of his career the young officer advanced himself by patronage (the befriendment of a senior officer in the service, usually the one who had found him his first commission). Seniority meant nothing to the up-and-coming young officer. This method of promotion prevailed up to the rank of commander, but as soon as post (captains) rank was reached the officer soon found out that seniority was the be-all and end-all. From now on he could not overtake the man ahead of him, and neither could he be passed over by a younger man. Owing to the Admiralty's policy of never retiring an officer, even if there was no ship or shore appointment for him, the end of every war and the decommissioning of large numbers of ships meant that large numbers of officers just stagnated on the rank they had reached, and 1815 was certainly no exception. As the fleet was quickly run down large numbers of officers commissioned for the war were simply placed on half pay. This of course meant that all promotions for more junior officers were thus blocked until the older ones died.

As a result the majority of commanding officers were often too old for their sea posts and few of the junior officers were senior enough in rank or had been given enough responsibility in the past to command these vessels.

Matters were, however, about to change. In 1815 the Admiralty instituted a policy whereby a board had to approve all new applicants for the post of midshipmen before they were appointed. This regulation of the numbers entering the commissioned ranks did to some extent alleviate the problem of too many officers in the service. As a side effect it also went part of the way towards sorting out many of those who would have proved unsuitable for positions of authority.

TABLE 1

Commissioned Officers in the Navy in December 1815

Flag Officers	220
Captains	860
Commanders	870
Lieutenants	Over 4200

TABLE 2

Ships in commission in 1814 and 1820

	1814	1820
Ships of the line	99	14
Frigate, sloops, brigs etc.	505	92

CHAPTER 2

Pax Britannica

. . . South, north, est and west,
Cherish marchaundyes, keep th'amiraltee,
That we be maysteres of the narrow sea
ADAM DE MOLEYNS
Bishop of Chichester

AS THE PRESSED MEN were gaining their freedom at the end of
the Napoleonic wars, the ships of the Royal Navy were engaged
in ensuring the freedom of another section of the community.
In February 1815 the Congress of Vienna outlawed the slave
trade (the British had already passed an act banning it in 1807)
and the navy at once set about implementing the act by searching
all vessels, irrespective of nationality, suspected of being involved
in the illegal trade and then freeing any slaves thus captured.
The main traffic in slaves took place from Africa, the poor
wretches being in the main transported to America or Asia from
west and east Africa. Huge sums of money were tied up in this
trade and many persons of high repute made huge fortunes from
it. The complete restriction placed on the slave traffic caused
not a few bankruptcies and suicides among these influential
people, but the navy continued with its task until the flow of
slaves out of Africa was but a mere trickle.

While the small sloops and frigates of the navy were engaged
in the suppression of the slave trade, yet other warships were
sent to break up the bands of Barbary Pirates that took a heavy
toll of merchant shipping along the north African coast. Piracy
in this region was organised on a massive scale and often State
backed. In order to enforce the new freedom of the seas Admiral
Edward Pellew took a squadron of warships to Algiers in 1816,
and bombarded the port, where hundreds of Europeans were
held in slavery. With the *Queen Charlotte* (100-guns) he took

with him the *Impregnable* (98-guns), three other ships of the line of 74-guns, one of 50-guns, four frigates, a few gunboats and a small squadron of Dutch frigates that had requested to accompany him.   This was a small squadron compared to the 25 ships-of-the-line that Nelson had estimated would be needed to reduce the port.   The force left Plymouth on July 28th, 1816, and after stopping at Gibraltar reached Algiers on August 27th, 1816.   There the Dey had assembled 40,000 men to oppose Admiral Pellew, who on arriving outside the port sent in an ultimatum which allowed the Dey two hours in which to surrender all slaves and return all plunder taken by the pirates. The Dey declined, and the British force sailed into pre-selected positions near the city, out of range of about half of the 1000 guns of the land batteries.   The flagship had just anchored about 100 yards from the pier when suddenly one of the land batteries opened fire.   At once three decks of guns from the *Queen Charlotte* replied, sweeping the mole that was dense with troops and killing, it was said, over 500 people.   Three broadsides were fired by the British, practically demolishing the town, and by ten o'clock the enemy batteries had been silenced, Admiral Pellew withdrawing his squadron.   The British losses were slight, 128 killed and about 700 wounded, while the Algerians lost over 7000.   The Dey surrendered at daybreak, apologising to the British Consul, paying an indemnity of 400,000 dollars and releasing over 3000 European slaves, none of whom proved to be British.   For his part in ridding the seas of the pirate menace Admiral Pellew was created Viscount Exmouth.   Although a few individual pirates persisted after the action, State backed piracy dwindled to almost nothing.

Although conditions in the service itself were poor, improvements were afoot in many other spheres.   The navy was not only responsible for protecting merchant shipping against unlawful attack, but also for ensuring the maritime safety of the sealanes.   For this the Royal Navy had been given a special commission to chart the oceans and coastlines of the world.   The hydrographic department of the navy had originally been formed in 1795, but not until the end of the Napeolonic wars were the survey ships really able to set about the enormous task of charting ocean currents, hazards such as shoals and wrecks and surveying multitudinous islands and coastlines.   Concurrent with this the

B

researches of the survey fleet began to be published under the direction of the hydrographer—Captain Thomas Hurd—in the Admiralty charts, which were then made available for all users of the high seas, and not exclusively for the Royal Navy as previously.

Captain Hurd was a man of great skill and under his guidance the navy undertook many surveys in different parts of the world as far apart as the West Indies, Sicily, Newfoundland and Great Britain herself. He is best remembered for his minutely detailed survey of the coast of Bermuda, a task which took him five years and hasn't been bettered since with modern scientific apparatus. Sir William Parry, the Arctic explorer, who succeeded Captain Hurd when he died in 1823, took over the twelve vessels which then formed the nucleus of the new survey fleet. For assistants Parry had Francis Beaufort, who took over the office of hydrographer when Parry resigned in 1829, and A. T. E. Vidal. Francis Beaufort, who remained in office for over 25 years, was knighted for his work which included a "Grand Survey of the British Isles" and the invention of the Beaufort wind scale.

More glamorous than the straightforward grind of charting currents and coastlines were the Polar expeditions undertaken by the Admiralty during the nineteenth century. Two such Arctic expeditions were fitted out in 1818 and although not proving very successful, did give valuable training to future leaders of such explorations. The first expedition set forth under Commander John Ross to attempt to find a North-West Passage. In command of the brig *Alexander* was another future leader and hydrographer of the Royal Navy—Lieutenant William Edward Parry.

The second expedition to sail was under command of Captain David Buchan who had with him yet another future explorer— Lieutenant John Franklin—who was in command of the *Trent*. Captain Buchan was attempting to reach the North Pole or its near neighbourhood but both ships in the squadron were severely damaged by the pack ice and failed to reach their objective.

The following year, 1819, two more expeditions were fitted out under Parry and Franklin. Parry sailed on May 11th with the *Hecla* and *Griper* in a further attempt to find a North West Passage. On September 4th he passed through 110°W and became entitled to the £5000 prize offered by the Government to any one who could penetrate so far to the west within the Arctic circle. Parry then decided to winter in the Arctic on Melville Island, the ships floating in May 1820 and finally breaking out on August 1st, having lost only one man out of the 94. Franklin led a far different expedition from that of Parry. Landing at Hudson Bay, Franklin's force journeyed overland to the mouth of the Coppermine River and then taking to their canoes on July 21st, 1821, they began to explore the Arctic coast eastwards covering a distance of 650 miles in atrocious weather conditions and suffering from a constant lack of provisions. Travelling back overland the party finally reached their base at Hudson Bay in June 1822.

Parry meanwhile was taking further expeditions north in attempts to find a North West Passage. In 1824 he lost his first vessel, the *Fury*, when she was so severely damaged by ice that she had to be abandoned. In April 1827 he set out on his last expedition to try and reach the North Pole by sledge from Spitzbergen, taking with him two 20-foot flat-bottomed boats. Sailing with Parry was Lieutenant James Clarke Ross, the nephew of Commander John Ross, three other officers and 24 men. After ice checked them the men took to the long boats, and travelling across the floes and on the water they journeyed for 35 days, until finally the southerly drift of ice forced them to abandon the attempt, and they finally planted the British flag in latitude 82°45' on July 26th, 1827.

The navy was not only ensuring the freedom of the seas passively, however, but actively as well. Suppression of the slave trade and piracy were two of the major roles performed by the navy officially, but unofficially it also became involved in a number of minor wars throughout the world, not only in the expansion of the British Empire but also, ironically, championing the self-determination of a number of weaker states against the big powers. Warships did not often participate in these struggles but men unofficially volunteered for service with these states. The first of the minor conflicts which men of the Royal Navy became involved in was the fighting between Spain and Portugal and their South American dependencies in 1818 lasting until 1825.

Soon after getting involved in the South American conflict

the navy went to the assistance of Portugal in 1820 and later a naval force was present at the capture of Rangoon on May 11th, 1824. A year after the Portuguese affair the First Lord of the Admiralty—Lord Melville—approved the purchase of a vessel— the *Monkey*—whose mode of propulsion was to revolutionise the Royal Navy. Built by William Elias Evans of Rotherhithe, the *Monkey* (212 tons) was a wooden-hulled tug propelled by paddles and driven by an 80HP steam engine. Steam had at long last entered the navy. The Admiralty purchased the *Monkey* as they realised that a steam tug with the ability to manouvre free of the wind would be most useful in handling sailing ships in confined spaces, such as harbours, where there was a great risk of grounding and being wrecked.

Steam was in its infancy, however, and prone to breakdown so its use in fighting ships was forbidden, in addition to which the cumbersome paddles used for propulsion would have meant a heavy sacrifice in broadside firepower. Although he had sanctioned the purchase of the *Monkey* in 1821 and the construction of the paddle steamer *Comet* (238 tons, 80HP) built by Oliver Lang at Deptford in 1822 for the mail packet service, Lord Melville was absolutely opposed to its general use in the navy. At one stroke it would mean the end of Britain's naval supremacy, rendering the whole of her sailing navy obsolete. It did this anyway, whether Lord Melville ordered steam vessels or not. Already the Admiralty was beginning to show its future policies of being utterly opposed to any changes taking place in the basic structure of the navy or its ships. The attitude was summed up in a statement made by Lord Melville in the autumn of 1828 when he replied to a query from the Colonial Office asking if the navy could employ steam vessels to carry the mails from Malta to Corfu, saying:

"Their Lordships feel it their bounden duty upon national and professional grounds to discourage to the utmost of their ability the employment of steam vessels, as they consider that the introduction of steam is calculated to strike a fatal blow at the naval supremacy of the Empire."

Not for seven years (from 1821 to 1828) was a steam vessel officially entered in the Navy Lists of vessels in commission, and in fact it wasn't until December 1827 that steam vessels were allowed to use the prefix HMS. The *Lightning* class (*Echo*,

Lightning and *Meteor*) were for the first time published in the List in January 1828.

Seeing the possibilities of steam the explorer Sir John Ross proposed to the Admiralty an Arctic expedition in 1827 using steam vessels. The Admiralty turned the suggestion down but Sir John carried on with his idea privately fitting out the paddle steamer *Victory* (whose engines in fact proved a failure). Leaving England in May 1829 he returned in October 1833, having discovered the North Magnetic Pole during his exploration and fixed it in latitude 70°5'17" longitude 96°46'45"W.

In 1821 an unsuccessful revolt in the Morea area of Greece signalled the commencement of the Greek war of independence. Having lived under Turkish rule since the mid-fifteenth century the Greeks now claimed independence from the Ottoman Empire. Fighting continued on and off for a number of years and aroused the interest of European powers. Among these was Great Britain who finally sent a combined squadron of British, French and Russian warships to the assistance of the Greeks. The Turks declined to accept recommendations from the great powers that they sign an armistice with Greece and so the combined British squadron under command of Vice-Admiral Sir Edward Codrington sailed in search of the combined Turkish and Egyptian fleets. The squadron consisted of three British, three French and four Russian ships of the line, four British and four Russian frigates and a number of smaller vessels. On October 27th, 1827, the Allied Squadron found the Turkish fleet anchored in the harbour at Navarino. The combined Egyptian and Turkish fleet comprised three ships of the line, 15 large frigates, 18 corvettes and a large number of lesser craft. Vice-Admiral Codrington sailed his squadron into the harbour where they anchored on the leeward side of the Turkish fleet. The Turks then opened fire on some of the allied squadron whereupon action was joined. The Turks were completely annihilated losing over 50 vessels and about 4000 men. Losses on the allied side were also heavy totalling 650 men, with the main British ships so severely damaged that they had to return to England for repairs. The battle was notable for two facts—it was the last battle between sailing ships of the line and was also the last time that Great Britain, France and Russia co-operated in a venture until 1915 and the Dardanelles campaign.

CHAPTER 3

The Paddle versus the Screw

*It is upon the Navy, under the good providence of
God, that the wealth, safety, and strength of the
Kingdom do chiefly depend*

THE ARTICLES OF WAR

BY 1830 many inventions were already threatening the very
existence of the Royal Navy, but those in charge were still slow
to accept new ideas. In the same year as the Battle of Navarino,
1827, a Frenchman by the name of Paixhans produced a new
projectile to be fired from cannon. This was the shell and its
incendiary capabilities immediately rendered every British warship a fireship. The shell was made up in a hollow canister
and filled with a charge of 4lb of gunpowder, the whole projectile
being the size of an 80lb shot. Having developed the shell,
Paixhans, determined that the French Navy would not be the
losers by it, promptly began experimenting to find a means of
defence against it.

The year 1830 proved to be quite an eventful year on the
naval scene. Apart from Paixhan's shell, which was being improved, a new design of an old invention by Archimedes was
under development. This was the screw. The few steam vessels
bought and built by the Royal Navy had, up until 1830, been
propelled by paddlewheels. Apart from the fact that their Lordships were opposed in general to the use of steam in warships,
paddlewheels prevented the vessels exploiting to the full the
possibilities of broadside fire, the ships losing a quarter and
sometimes a third of their broadside batteries. With the screw
placed in the water under the stern of the vessel the huge
encumbrance of the paddle amidships would allow vessels to
regain their full broadside armament. The use of the screw

22

could give the navy the supremacy it had begun to lose. Two great advantages would accrue from the use of the screw—freedom of movement to develop to the full maximum firepower on any chosen target, and greater protection for the propulsive unit. Paddlewheels were open to destruction from one well aimed shot but a screw underwater would be practically indestructible.

With Paixhans' new shell springing into prominence it was only natural that gunnery came to be looked upon more as a science than an art, as hitherto practised. Thus in 1830 Commander George Smith commissioned a new establishment for the Royal Navy. The new establishment was the School of Gunnery which Commander Smith set up on board a ship of the line moored in Portsmouth harbour. The vessel used was the *Queen Charlotte*, the 74-gun flagship of Admiral Pellew at the bombardment of Algiers. On being commissioned for the School of Gunnery she was renamed HMS *Excellent*. This was the first Naval Technical School formed by the Royal Navy and in Commander Smith's own words it was set up to enable "gunners to learn one general and perfect system of gunnery, not only to be able to give the words of command, but more particularly to see they are executed as they ought to be".

At first the training of gunners was fairly straightforward, as the guns were still smooth-bore muzzle-loaders mainly of 32-pdr size. With the coming of the shell a number of 32-pdrs had been bored to eight or ten inches to take the projectile, but as it remained spherical for a while no problems were encountered, and a ship normally carried a mixed armament of shot and shell firing guns. Usually the gun deck carried the shell firing guns and the batteries above the 32-pdr shot firing ones. It wasn't until later that gunnery really became complex, when many different sizes and type of guns entered service with different operational requirements. Then the gunners, like the engineers in charge of the steam engines, gained recognition as a seaman branch of their own, with special training. Already though the conditions in the navy were becoming such that it was impossible for an ordinary seaman to encompass all the sailor's duties on a ship-of-the-line as previously.

Towards the end of 1830 great changes occurred in the Board of Admiralty. Sir James Graham replaced Lord Melville as First Lord and Sir Thomas Masterman Hardy (Nelson's old captain) was appointed First Sea Lord. Hardy on assuming office realised the precarious state of the navy and at once set about redressing some of the shortsighted policies carried out by his predecessors. For a start he saw that the era of the sailing ship was coming to an end, and he was a firm believer in steam, but had to convince many others in the Admiralty and the navy who were sceptics. He also realised what a potent projectile Paixhans' new shell could be. One way of improving vessels of the Royal Navy already in service was to increase their mobility. Ever since Nelson's time, and long before that, the method of fighting was to lay your vessel alongside the enemy, firing broadsides continuously and board him. To this end the Admirals had called for heavier and heavier broadsides until a ship-of-the-line in 1830 normally carried between 60 and 74 guns, often 100 and in some cases even as many as 130 guns. As a start to increasing the mobility and reducing weight Hardy removed many of the batteries on these vessels, converting them into 50 gun frigates. Lord Melville's pride and joy, the 46 gun frigates, were removed from the fleet or converted into much handier corvettes, while the almost useless sloops and brigs were scrapped altogether. What Hardy was doing in fact was to create a new navy. The heavy broadside was still essential, however, and so Hardy set out to have new ships designed which would mount new guns in as heavy a broadside as possible, but still retaining manouverability.

The ships themselves, however, were not Hardy's only concern. For years the dockyards had been a disgrace. Corruption was rife, especially among the victuallers. These men often supplied food that was unfit even for animal consumption, let alone the hardworking crews of ships. The process of canning had been developed, but even here malpractices occurred. It had even been known for a tin of canned meat to contain nothing but a pressed horse's hoof.

The other direction in which Hardy tried to make improvements was in the question of promotion. He realised that the method of promoting senior officers was causing a complete blockage for the younger and abler officers, of which the navy, with its gradual process of modernisation was in great need. Officers who had served in the Napoleonic wars were still on the active list. In 1825 for example there was a total of 5539 commissioned officers of which only 550 had active posts; 90% were unemployed and of this total, 205 were flag officers of which only ten were in service. 95% were unemployed.

Very gradually, however, conditions in all spheres of the navy improved, but not without their quota of mistakes. In 1832 the surveyor of the Royal Navy resigned and was replaced by a Captain William Symonds. Captain Symonds had taught himself the mechanics of sailing ship design and construction, but knew nothing about steam engines, nor was he really anxious to appraise himself of their capabilities. This was unfortunate as in 1834, the year that Hardy's term as First Sea Lord came to an end, a certain Edward Berthon presented the Admiralty with a three-foot model of a screw vessel driven by a two-bladed propeller. The Admiralty was not impressed, however, and Captain Symonds continued to build wooden sailing vessels fitted with auxiliary steam engines to drive the paddles. Next Francis Pettit Smith tried to convince the Admiralty of the need for screw propulsion, patenting a screw propeller in May 1836, followed six weeks later by a Swede, John Ericsson, who also patented a model. Ericsson was also rebuffed and went to live in America. Smith was more successful than either Berthon or Ericsson, actually building a demonstration vessel of ten tons powered by a 6HP engine. This vessel was seen by many Londoners as it steamed up and down the Paddington Canal. After a short spell on the Thames, Smith took his boat to the coast in September 1837, where the Admiralty observed its progress. At last a glimmer of light shone in their minds and they asked Smith to construct a larger vessel. Thus in April 1837 the *Francis B. Ogden* was launched on the Thames and their Lordships invited to try out the new screw vessel.

It was decided to test the capabilities of the new ship by making her tow the Admiralty Barge down the Thames from Somerset House to Blackwall. The day of the experiment dawned and the most impressive assembly of naval officers yet seen gathered together to witness an experiment duly boarded the Barge at Somerset House. The party included Captain Symonds the surveyor, Captain Francis Beaufort the hydrographer, Rear-Admiral Sir Charles Adam the First Sea Lord, and the Arctic explorer and navigator Captain Sir Edward Parry. The round trip from Somerset House to Blackwall and back was completed without incident, the Barge being towed along at an average speed of from nine to ten knots.

The man for whose benefit the experiment was really being made, however, was not impressed in the slightest. The only remark he could make at the end of the trip was, that as the screw was at the stern of the vessel she would be incapable of being steered properly, and this after she had just towed the Admiralty Barge down the Thames.

Smith, however, was not to be put off. His next effort at persuading the Admiralty to adopt screw propulsion was far more successful. After his previous rebuff he set to work to build a much larger steamer with the help of a company which he managed to form. The new vessel was powered by an 80HP engine and displaced 237 tons. Named *Archimedes*, she was shown to the Admiralty in 1839 at Sheerness where she was put through her paces at nine knots. This was not sufficient for the Admiralty who wanted to see a much more convincing test, especially as all the steamers then in the navy were paddlers. So it was that the *Archimedes* was taken to Portsmouth, home of the Royal Navy, and sailed against the fastest paddler in the navy—the *Vulcan*.

The *Vulcan* was convincingly beaten, but still the admirals were not satisfied. By now there was only one other vessel in Great Britain against whom the *Archimedes* could be matched. This was the merchant vessel *Widgeon*. As Captain Edward Chappell, who was appointed to make reports on the tests pointed out, there was a marked difference in tonnage between the vessels (*Archimedes* 237 tons, *Widgeon* 192 tons) and also in motive power (*Archimedes* 80HP, *Widgeon* 90HP).

Naturally the *Widgeon* showed up better in the tests than the *Archimedes*, but Captain Chappell emphasised in his report that the power of the screw vessel was at least on a par with that of the paddle, if not superior. However, this was still not the deciding factor.

In the meantime while all the wrangling was in progress over the use of screw propulsion, events had been steadily moving to a climax with Paixhans' shell. In 1830 he had suggested a method of defence against his new projectile. Wooden warships, he stated, should be constructed with a belt of iron round the hull which ought to be between seven and eight inches thick.

To compensate for this great increase in weight one deck of guns would have to be dispensed with. As a result of the introduction of the new shell and the resulting need for extra protection the Admiralty commenced experiments in this direction, and in 1838 carried out a series of trials at Woolwich with the old three-decker sailing vessel *Prince George*. Included in the experiments were a number of tests designed to find out the effect of shellfire against new materials, such as a new preparation known as kamptulicon. This consisted of a mixture of cork and india rubber which formed the inside lining of iron plates which were riveted together, the lining being kept in place by wood packing. It was thought, and hoped, that when shells passed through the kamptulicon it would close up and form a watertight seal. This it did, but the iron tended to splinter with such adverse effect that its use was discouraged. The problem of whether to build ships of iron or wood was further accentuated by the results obtained from the wooden vessels converted to steam propulsion. These were beginning to show signs of strain from the vibrations of the engines.

CHAPTER 4

Iron enters the Navy

Bear in mind the necessity of maintaining the
sovereignty of the seas, whereon the peace, plenty
and prosperity of the Island depend
LORD HUNGERFORD
The Libell of Englische Policye, 1436

THE ADVENT of the steam engine proved too much for wooden
vessels, and the excessive vibrations that resulted caused timbers
in the hulls to spring and leaks to occur. Generally the vessels
were rather poor sea boats and very cramped for space, not
proving as satisfactory in service as had been hoped. Following
the experiments of Paixhans and the tests on the old *Prince
George*, the Admiralty had been building composite vessels of
wooden hulls protected by iron belts. The next step was to
build a vessel completely of iron. This would give the necessary
strength to the hull and enable the vessel to mount the more
powerful steam engines that were then under design. It would
also provide extra protection against shell fire. The new plans
proved unpopular among the general public, however, and such
was the outcry in the press that the Admiralty was forced to
reconsider its decision to build iron vessels. A number were
already in service though, the first being the screw steamer
Mermaid (164 tons) bought in 1842 and renamed *Dwarf*. Prior
to the purchase of the *Mermaid* the Admiralty had been advised
to construct iron vessels with a view to protecting them from the
devastating effect of Paixhans' new shell. This was necessary as
a number of foreign navies had already adopted the new shell.
William Laird, who had pioneered the construction of iron
merchants ships, had drawn up plans for such an iron frigate in
1836, but they had been turned down by the Admiralty.
With the purchase of the *Mermaid* the Admiralty also placed

an order for seven iron ships, the first of which, the *Trident* (1850 tons, 300HP), was completed at Blackwall in 1843. She was followed two years later by a further order for five frigates (the largest being 1953 tons), and six lightly armed steam tenders. The surveyor, however, was not at all happy about these orders. He had had some reservations about accepting steam, which he had overcome, but iron ships and armour plate would, as he pointed out to the Admiralty, "occupy so much space and involve so enormous an increase of weight as to render the adoption of them entirely out of the question in her Majesty's steam vessels". His statements were, however, only made upon the results of the tests that had been carried out by the Admiralty. These results had shown that when subjected to the fire of solid shot, jagged lengths of iron had been torn off. As Paixhans' shells had not been used in the tests the results were inconclusive. Ordinary iron had been used and only subjected to the fire of round shot. Armour plate, such as Paixhans had suggested should be used for protection against his shells had not been tested, and the experiments had been conducted against a small steamer, the 73-ton *Ruby*. For the tests she had been anchored as a stationary target and subjected to a carefully directed fire from a 32-pdr and 8-inch gun. The shot so ruptured the framing and plates of the vessel, that in the official report of Captain Chads, who observed the tests, "the shot meets with so little resistance that it must inevitably go through the vessel, and should it strike on a rib on the opposite side the effect is terrific, tearing off the iron sheets to a very considerable extent; and even those shot that go clean through the fracture being on the off side, the rough edges are outside the vessel, precluding the possibility almost of stopping them". Realising the future trend of gunnery development and tactics Captain Chads fired the shot at the vessel from the end-on position (crossing the "T") and reported that, "each shot cut away the ribs and, tearing the iron plates away, would be sufficient to sink the vessel in an instant". The trials continued, but the results were still discouraging, the shot causing large holes with extremely irregular and jagged edges, making plugging exceedingly difficult and if occurring near the waterline giving rise to a very dangerous situation. As a report in 1849 stated, "shot of every description in passing through iron makes such large holes that the material is improper for the bottom of ships".

Apart from this there was the possibility of extreme destruction caused to the guns crews by the disintegration of the shot behind the iron plates. This led Captain Chads to a conclusion in his report of 1850 that, "from these circumstances I am confirmed in the opinion that iron cannot be beneficially employed as a material for the construction of vessels of war". This at once sealed the fate of the iron ships.

The iron frigates that had already been built could not be scrapped without a great waste of money and so they were all converted to troopships under the order of the First Lord, the Earl of Auckland—George Eden. One of these iron troopships, the *Birkenhead*, gained notoriety when she sank in 1852 off South Africa with the loss of 432 soldiers. Seventeen other iron frigates were under construction at the time and were scrapped or converted, the largest being the *Simoom* of 2000 tons.

The construction of iron frigates was not the only advance attempted in 1845. Up until then the only steamer accepted by the Admiralty was the paddle vessel. A 46-gun frigate, the *Penelope*, had been cut in half and had a 65-foot middle added with 650HP engines driving paddles which gave her a speed of 10 knots. An indication of the space required by the steam engines is shown in the number of guns which were removed. After conversion to a paddler the total number of guns carried was 16. Following Captain Chappel's report on the experiments between the *Archimedes* and the *Widgeon* the Admiralty decided to carry out a much fairer trial of strength between the screw and the paddle. To ensure fair conditions, vessels of identical tonnage and horsepower were needed and it was decided to requisition two sloops for the experiment. The vessels chosen were the *Alecto*, a paddle vessel of 200HP and a screw vessel the *Rattler*. The *Rattler* had originally been laid down by Captain Symonds as the sailing sloop *Ardent* of 880 tons. Under the influence of Captain Chappel's report, however, Captain Symonds fitted the *Ardent* with a Pettit Smith two-bladed propeller and launched her in April 1843 under the name *Rattler*. On the day of the experiment the two vessels were lashed stern to stern and when everything was ready both were simultaneously given the signal to steam full ahead. At first nothing happened but then very gradually the *Rattler* began to move ahead, slowly quickening pace until she was towing the *Alecto* along at a steady 2½ knots.

This experiment finally convinced the Admiralty, and in 1844 they placed an order for a screw frigate—the *Dauntless*. The *Dauntless* was preceded by a screw frigate conversion—the *Amphion*, converted while still on the stocks and launched in 1846. Following these vessels a number of ships-of-the-line were converted to screw propulsion while still on the stocks in 1850. These conversions were completed only just in time as the French designer, Dupuy de Lôme, who had toured British shipyards studying construction methods and techniques, had returned home and was trying to convince Napoleon III that the only answer to British naval supremacy was to construct screw propelled iron ships protected by armour plate. Napoleon wasn't fully convinced of the feasibility of the idea, but De Lôme went ahead with an idea of his own and constructed the *Napoleon*, a 92-gun wooden ship-of-the-line. Her main feature was a 960HP engine which drove a screw to give her a speed of $13\frac{3}{4}$ knots. As soon as they received the news of the construction of the *Napoleon* the Admiralty lost no time in ordering a British ship-of-the-line specially designed for screw propulsion. Launched at Woolwich in May 1852 she was named *Agamemnon*.

By the time the *Agamemnon* was launched, Sir William Symonds was no longer surveyor of the Royal Navy. During his term of office he had had large numbers of vessels constructed, especially in the frigate rate, and did much to redress the imbalance that had built up between the Royal Navy and the French, who were still looked upon as the only potential enemy. For a number of years commanding officers had been sending reports to the Admiralty complaining of the excessive rolling experienced in the vessels designed by Captain Symonds. Due to the large number of complaints a committee was assembled in 1846 with the commission to form a judgement upon the designs of Captain Symonds. He had pinned his faith in paddle steamers, and during his term of office over 200 of them had been constructed for the navy. Rather than be subjected to a public examination of his work by the committee Captain Symonds preferred to resign from the navy. He was responsible for the introduction of a number of innovations into the ships of the Royal Navy and although he may not have been a keen supporter of steam propulsion or iron vessels, due mainly to his ignorance of their technicalities, he did make improvements to the designs of warships. Perhaps the main difference came about as a result of the racing yachts he had built before he became surveyor. He applied the designs of the fine lines of the yachts to the hulls of the vessels he designed for the Admiralty, so improving their underwater characteristics that they could reach a speed of 13 knots (as much as the steam propelled vessels at that time) and were far easier to sail. This did, however, tend to make the vessels rather lively, giving rise to the rolling motion of which so many captains complained. He also made adjustments to the designs of the bows and sterns of sailing vessels, strengthening them against end-on fire.

CHAPTER 5

The Crimean War

Wherever there is water to float a ship, we are sure to find you in the way

NAPOLEON

THE COMMENCEMENT of the Crimean War in October 1853, when Turkey declared war on Russia, heralded many changes throughout the world. It was the first full-scale war since 1815 and both the Royal Navy and the Army became fully embroiled in the conflict. The start of the war found the navy wanting in many respects; only a few ships-of-the-line had been fitted with screw propulsion, and these were all conversions and still carried their sails; and all the iron frigates had been relegated to troopships on the orders of the First Lord. Not a single iron ship existed in the navy! Recruitment, however, was now a much more organised affair, as a year before, in 1852, the Admiralty had set up a new system of entry for the lower deck. This was an immediate success, as for the first time a man joined the navy with the knowledge that in ten years he could leave the service. The new system of continuous service was aimed at the younger man who was invited to volunteer for the service at the age of eighteen, when he would sign on for ten years. With the start of the Crimean War the new long-term service engagements became much more important with the need for large numbers of men. Although recruiting figures improved, the sudden commissioning of large numbers of ships for the Crimean War still left the navy undermanned. The main advantage of the long-term engagement was that it gave the navy time to train a man properly in his job, and when he retired from the service he formed part of the Fleet Reserve and could be called up in an emergency. With the new complex branch structure of the

Royal Navy the merchant seaman, who had always formed the reserve of manpower for the fleet, no longer had a place, except as an ordinary seaman. So in 1859 a new reserve, called the Royal Naval Reserve, was formed which allowed a merchant seaman to volunteer for service with the Royal Navy on a part-time basis when he was given practical training in the new branches.

Although at the start of the Crimean War the ships of the Royal Navy were in a rather poor state, the crews were in a high state of efficiency. On November 30th, 1853, a month after the opening of the war the Russian Fleet completely destroyed a Turkish Squadron of seven frigates at the Battle of Sinope. This battle was highly significant in naval history as for the first time Paixhans' new shell had been used in action, by the Russians. The French and British watched the battle with great interest before forming an alliance and declaring war in March 1854. Emperor Napoleon III had been so impressed with the outcome of the battle that he at once told his naval constructor Mr. Dupuy de Lôme that he could go ahead, under government support, and build an iron-plated vessel. Napoleon had realised that the wooden sailing ship-of-the-line was finished and so enthusiastic did he become about warships that he at once set about drawing up plans himself. One of his designs was for a heavily armoured battery that would float very low in the water to minimise the effect of shell fire. The plans for the new battery were sent to the Admiralty, who after some delay ordered four similar vessels, the *Glatton*, *Meteor*, *Thunder* and *Trusty*.

Apart from the Battle of Sinope there were no major fleet actions during the war, operations consisting in the main of blockading the Russians in their ports. Odessa was bombarded by frigates in April 1854 and in September of that year a British force of ten ships-of-the-line, two frigates and thirteen armed merchant cruisers commenced the blockade of Sevastopol, after convoying a Turkish Army for an attack on the port. The Russians refused to sortie and in order to avoid being captured scuttled their fleet in the harbour. The allied blockade then began with a bombardment of the port which continued sporadically for some weeks. The sailing ships-of-the-line, which were towed into position by steam tugs, became sitting targets for the guns of the fortress and suffered considerable damage. The few vessels that had auxiliary engines fared little better. The few real steam vessels available, however, showed their worth from the start, their complete freedom of movement giving them the ability to manoeuvre out of range of the Russian batteries. The effort was doomed to failure from the start though.

Baltic operations during the Crimean War were of little note. Under Admiral Sir Charles Napier a British squadron bombarded Sveaborg and blockaded the Russians behind their fortifications at Kronstadt, from whence they floated mines against the British. This was the first time that mines had been used at sea, but they failed to cause any material damage to the British, neither did they force them to raise the blockade. The mines themselves were spherical in shape and filled with 70lb of explosive, while projecting from the casing were horns in which were placed glass phials of sulphuric acid. The horn on making contact with an object broke the phial, the sulphuric acid igniting chlorate of potash. In spite of the menace of the mines the British squadron continued to bombard Kronstadt having little effect against the strong fortifications. Apart from this hazard the Baltic squadron was also bedevilled by a shortage of seamen, many of the crews being supplemented by volunteers from the Scandinavian countries.

It was slowly being realised that apart from the ships being in a poor state materially, through being laid up in reserve, they were also the wrong type of ship for these operations. The waters around the Russian ports in the Baltic and Black Sea were very shallow and the ships-of-the-line just could not get near enough to the forts for fear of grounding. What was needed was a large number of boats of very shallow draught carrying one or two large guns. Admiral Napier had already pointed this out to the First Lord in a letter dated July 18th, 1854, where he referred to the only successful way of attacking Sveaborg as by, "fitting out a great number of gunboats, carrying one gun with a long range".

The only vessels suitable for the job were six vessels of the *Arrow* class, originally completed as dispatch vessels, but re-rated as sloops. These were armed with two of the new Lancaster 68-pdr muzzle-loaders. As a result of the pressing needs for this type of vessel the Admiralty ordered six more vessels capable of mounting two 68-pdr guns with shallow draft. This led to the design of the *Gleaner* class of wooden-hulled gunboats, relying mainly on steam engines driving a single screw for propulsion, but with provision for sails, as there was not sufficient bunkerage aboard for a long voyage. The class proved ideal in service and orders were placed for a further twenty vessels of the *Dapper* class of almost similar design. A small flotilla of gunboats was then formed for use in the Sea of Azov and provided invaluable service attacking depots, troop concentrations, railheads and generally causing havoc. Others in the new class took part in the second bombardment of Sveaborg in August 1855 with notable success. As a result of these successful operations the order for the *Dapper* class of gunboats was increased to a total of 98.

Under the Franco-British Alliance representatives from British shipyards went to France to see over the dockyards and inspect the progress in naval construction in France. At one place, plans for the use of armour plate were inspected but the British were unconvinced of its practicability. Neither was the First Lord, Sir James Graham, convinced, and before expending vast sums of money on ordering armour plate he decided to have tests made. These were carried out against plates 9ft by 15in by $4\frac{1}{2}$in thick which were bolted to a wood backing of fir 4in thick, the whole being fixed to butts. Against this target a 32-pdr gun fired solid shot from a range of 360 yards. On impact the shot completely disintegrated and the plate was only dented, even a 68-pdr fired at a range of 900 yards failed to damage it. As a result of these tests this composite construction was recommended for the new type of gunboats and small warships then being designed.

By 1855 the first of Napoleon's batteries was ready and immediately vindicated the faith placed in them. Built of wood they displaced 1400 tons and carried eighteen 50-pdr guns protected by 4in armour plate, and were manned by a crew of 320. They were in action almost at once at the Battle of Kinburn in October 1855. During the battle the batteries were floated up to the fortress where they suffered numerous hits, one battery having two men killed and 13 wounded, and a second nine wounded. In spite of being hit over 137 times by 24-pdr shot these two batteries suffered no material damage whatsoever, and completely destroyed the enemy forts. Following the success of the French batteries the First Sea Lord at once ordered work to commence on the construction of a further four (the *Aetna, Erebus, Terror* and *Thunderbolt*) for the Royal Navy. The first, the *Aetna*, carrying sixteen 68-pdr guns was laid down in the naval dockyard at Chatham in November 1855 and her final cost turned out to be more than £50,000, as much as a three-deck ship-of-the-line. The other three vessels were ordered from private yards, but before any of them could be completed the Crimean War ended. The *Aetna* was commissioned and sent to Sheerness as a police vessel while a second sailed to Bermuda. The remaining two vessels were never commissioned, the *Erebus* being used in firing tests in 1858.

Apart from the Crimean War the Admiralty had further pressing matters on its mind in 1855. It had been decided to standardise the uniform of the seaman, as at the time many various forms of dress were in use, depending on the whim of each vessel's commanding officer. A committee was appointed under Rear-Admiral the Hon. Henry John Rous with orders to plan a new uniform. After studying all the variations then in use the committee put forward a proposal for a uniform of frock white duck with two rows of tape on the collar. Before accepting the idea, however, it was decided to place it before the Commanders-in-Chief of the two naval bases—Portsmouth and Devonport, who in turn put the proposals before each of the captains under their command. The majority favoured three rows of white tape $\frac{3}{16}$in wide and space $\frac{1}{8}$in apart. This was formally accepted, and on January 31st, 1857, the Admiralty requested every seaman to modify his dress accordingly.

In 1855 a Mr. Armstrong of Elswick began experiments with a new type of gun that he had built from a design prepared by a Mr. Longridge. The construction was revolutionary for instead of casting the barrel as a single unit it was made by shrinking a series of wrought iron tubes wound round with wire onto an inner barrel. This ensured that the inner barrel would be free from the strain due to whipping when the gun was fired. In addition the inside of the inner barrel was rifled and instead of being muzzle loaded was charged from the breech. The new gun immediately altered the whole course of gunnery. The novel feature of the gun was, of course, its breech mechanism which gave it an amazing rapidity of fire compared with the old muzzle loaders. It was also designed to fire Paixhans' shell which had now developed from its round shot to an elongated shape with a pointed head. This, together with a row of studs sited at the flat base of the shell that engaged in the rifling of the barrel when fired, resulted in a remarkable accuracy not obtained before. The race was now on between the gun and armour. The new gun underwent its first test in January 1859, too late to have any effect on the Crimean War. Although the tests proved the gun to be somewhat of a failure large numbers of Armstrong's gun were ordered for the navy, the sizes being 110-pdr, 40-pdr, 20-pdr, 12-pdr and 6-pdr.

Not only was Armstrong experimenting with guns, for the engineering works of Mr. Whitworth at Manchester received a number of 24-pdr guns from Woolwich in April 1856. The guns were bored out and rifled and experiments carried out with various types of shell. Although basically cast as a 24-pdr the gun was only bored to fire a 9lb shot. The projectiles were again the new Paixhans' elongated shell. Although only bored to fire the equivalent of a 9lb shot the new gun could fire shells of 24, 32, and 48lbs, the increased charge being obtained by increasing the length of the shell. The Whitworth gun was tested in October 1858 by Captain Hewlett of HMS *Excellent*. A 68-pdr fired wrought iron shot at the *Alfred*, the 4in iron plates of the vessel being penetrated and the 7in oak side behind being pierced. Unfortunately the gun exploded on firing. In spite of its tendency to burst the gun formed the standard armament of many of the gunboats until it fell into disfavour from this fault.

Alongside these startling new developments the old standard 32-pdr was also improved. By the end of the Crimean War it had been fitted with a flintlock firing mechanism and had a crude sighting arrangement. An attempt was made to improve the truck carriage of the gun, but only a few examples of the Marshall slide carriage as it was known, were introduced for the stern- and bow-chasers.

As a result of the experiments with the new types of gun it was decided to evolve a new system of nomenclature for gun sizes. Instead of referring to a gun by the weight of shot that it fired it was agreed to size the gun by calibres.

As the Crimean War drew to an end in February 1856 the French managed to complete a number of small armoured steamers. Basically these were wooden steam vessels that had been covered with 4½in iron plates, which proved in action to be impenetrable to the Russian shells. Not long after this, however, Franco-British relations began to deteriorate again and war was almost declared in January 1858 when an Italian refugee living in London attempted to assassinate Emperor Napoleon III. Matters were serious as by then the French Navy had made up the losses suffered at Trafalgar and the number and quality of their ships equalled those of the Royal Navy (29 steam line-of-battle ships) their steam frigates actually being superior to their British counterparts.

Forced into a compromising position the Admiralty formed a committee at the end of 1858 under Lord Derby with the commission, "to consider the very serious increase which had taken place of late years in the Navy Estimates while it represented that the naval force of the country is far inferior to what it ought to be with reference to that of other Powers, and especially France, and that increased efforts and increased expenditure were imperatively called for to place it on a proper footing".

After due deliberation the committee recommended that 19 line-of-battle ships should at once be converted into steam vessels, and Sir John Pakington made provision for these in the Spring Estimates of 1859. Plans were made to develop Armstrong's new gun, hoping that this would also help to give the Royal Navy superiority over the French. Meanwhile in May 1858 news had reached the Admiralty that two frigates of a new design were under construction at Toulon. Events were gathering pace as the following month it was learnt that one of these frigates was to have an iron belt to protect her side timbers. The latest vessel under construction for the navy was the wooden sailing vessel *Victoria*. The *Victoria* was built to the same design as previous ships-of-the-line, carrying 121 guns, and was fitted with auxiliary steam machinery. But serious doubts about the wisdom of building more wooden vessels now began to assail those in charge at the Admiralty.

Although by 1857 the Crimean War had shown the futility of the continued construction of wooden warships, there were only 58 iron vessels in the Royal Navy, comprised of small gunboats, mortar boats and miscellaneous auxiliaries. No iron vessels larger than a gunboat had been built mainly as a result of the tests carried out on the iron steamer *Ruby* (see end of previous chapter). In all between 1854 and 1857 only one vessel in five completed was of iron. The main backbone of the Royal Navy remained the three-deck sailing vessel, such as the *Victoria*, fitted with auxiliary steam machinery.

In the meantime the navy had been engaged in further hostilities. In the same year as peace was signed with Russia fighting broke out in China. Although not developing into full-scale war these incidents did involve the majority of warships in the Far East. The fighting arose because, it was claimed, the Chinese had broken the conditions of a treaty signed in 1842. The opening action of the Second China War began when a British squadron under Rear-Admiral Sir Michael Seymour, the C-in-C on the China Station, captured the port of Canton on October 25th, 1856, but was forced to abandon it soon after due to a lack of troops.

The following June Admiral Seymour tried again, this time with gunboats newly arrived from England. With a force of two paddle steamers, seven gunboats and numerous smaller craft he attacked a Chinese force of about 70 armed junks in Fatshan Creek. The Chinese force was utterly destroyed.

In between the major actions the gunboats and sloops were continually chasing roving bands of pirate junks.

The next major action occurred in May 1858. The scene had shifted to the Peiho River where a combined British and French force were attempting to reach Peking. The entrance to the Peiho River was guarded by a series of heavily defended forts at Taku. The first object was to demolish the mud forts which were bombarded by a small force of gunboats on May 20th, 1858. With the Taku forts in allied hands the way was open for the forcing of Tientsin. The squadron had by then been reinforced by more gunboats and the presence of the force outside the walls of Tientsin had a profound effect on the population. Soon after, on June 27th, a treaty was signed, but unfortunately it did not end the war, and trouble broke out again in April 1859. Admiral Seymour had now been replaced by Rear-Admiral Sir James Hope and he at once set about forcing the Peiho River with a squadron of ten gunboats and a sloop. Again a series of forts—the Peiho Forts—blocked the way. The force became trapped in a narrow channel and was repulsed with the loss of three gunboats, Admiral Hope being severely wounded. Peace was finally achieved in August the following year when Admiral Hope recaptured the Taku Forts, Tientsin and finally Peking, where the Summer Palace was sacked to force the Chinese to ratify the peace agreement.

While the Second China War was in progress the secretary to the Admiralty, Henry Thomas Lowry Corry, requested in June 1858 that two or more iron belted frigates should be built for the Royal Navy under the 1859 Estimates. In that same month the surveyor to the navy, Wake-Walker, set out the Admiralty's policy in a statement in which he said, "Although I have frequently stated it is not in the interest of Great Britain, possessing as she does so large a navy, to adopt any important change in the construction of ships of war which might have the effect of rendering necessary the introduction of a new class of very costly vessels, until such a course if forced upon her by the adoption of Foreign Powers of formidable ships of a novel character requiring similar ships to cope with them, yet it becomes a matter not only of expediency but of absolute necessity".

Finally in February 1859 the First Lord, fully appraised of French progress, agreed to the necessity for ironclads, stating that, "it is our duty to lose no time in building at least two". Following this a contract was placed for the first British ironclad in May 1859. Then in June the First Lord's term of office came to an end before the second vessel could be ordered. In October the first ironclad was named *Warrior* and the second, which had by then been ordered, *Invincible*.

This was not a moment too soon as on November 24th, 1859, the French launched the first of their new frigates—*La Gloire*—at Toulon. She at once caused a complete furore in naval circles. Basically her hull was that of the *Napoleon*, but, and here was her secret, it was protected by armour plates 5ft by 2ft by 4½in thick. She was rigged with three masts, as in previous ships, but the area of sail carried was very much reduced. *La Gloire* relied mainly on her steam engines for propulsion and the sails were carried just for emergencies, in case the engines should break down. She carried enough fuel to remain at sea for a month cruising at a speed of eight knots and her maximum speed was 13 knots on a displacement of 5600 tons. Finally in December 1860 the *Warrior* was launched. Designed by the

Chief constructor Isaac Watts and John Scott Russell the Admiralty had staked the whole future of the navy on the *Warrior* and her sister ship *Invincible*, by then renamed *Black Prince*. (This had been occasioned when it was learnt that the French had just launched an ironclad named *Invincible*). This policy paid off. Compared to *La Gloire* the *Warrior* was a much larger and superior vessel. Although constructed completely of iron and protected by an armour belt 4½in thick which extended for three-fifths of her length amidships, protecting the 1250NHP engine which drove the single screw, the Admiralty could still not bring themselves to do away with sailing vessels and so the *Warrior* retained a full rig. Sails, however, did give the navy a tremendous advantage, in that the vessels so rigged were independent of foreign bases for fuel supplies.

Although the Admiralty had provided the *Warrior* with an armoured belt, none was provided along the waterline and her steering gear was vulnerable to the first well aimed shot. There was extra protection, however, in the form of internal sub-divisions, there being 92 watertight compartments. As originally built the *Warrior* mounted twenty-six smooth-bore 68-pdr guns, of which four forward and four aft were unprotected, and ten 110-pdr and four 70-pdr Armstrong BLR guns. This armament was later altered to twenty-eight 7in MLR, four 8in MLR and four 20-pdr BLR guns.

CHAPTER 6

The Ironclad Navy

*It will always be said of us with unabated reverence
"they built ships of the line"*

JOHN RUSKIN
Harbours of England

WITH THE LAUNCHING of the *Warrior* at Blackwall in 1860 the
Royal Navy entered the arms race of the nineteenth century.
Improvements in equipment were evolving so rapidly that almost
before a new type of ship was launched she was obsolete. In
the same year that the *Warrior* was launched a body of men
formed themselves into an association that was to have a profound effect on the design and construction of warships. Under
the chairmanship of John Scott Russell, men like Dr. Woolley,
headmaster of the school of mathematics and naval construction
at Portsmouth, Edward J. Reed and Nathaniel Barnaby his
brother-in-law, who were to be responsible for the construction
of the new iron navy, and others created the Institute of Naval
Architects.

Having become a member of the Institute, Reed placed before
the Admiralty plans he had drawn up for an ironclad. He had
already submitted similar plans for a fast armoured frigate as
long ago as 1854, but they had been rejected. From the second
set of drafts, plans were made to convert three wooden vessels
into ironclads with a waterline armour belt and the main
armament protected by an armoured central citadel. Work on
the conversions, the *Enterprise, Favourite* and *Research* began in
1862. The First Lord, the Duke of Somerset, was so impressed
with Reed's work and ideas that when Isaac Watts the Chief
Constructor retired at the beginning of 1863 Reed was appointed
to the post. Reed's conception of the ironclad was of a com-

pletely new type of vessel whose merits were, "Possessing great powers of offence and defence, being comparatively short, cheap, and handy, and steaming at a high speed . . . by means of a moderate increase of power on account of the moderate proportions adopted . . .".

The Royal Navy was kept fully employed during the 1860's ensuring that the Pax Britannica was enforced. Although at peace with China the small gunboats of the navy were kept busy chasing pirates and engaged in actions against groups of rebel Chinese who were at variance with the policies of the Peking Government. Such a large group of rebels were the Taepings who were in action with a number of gunboats between 1860 and 1862.

Apart from further incidents in China vessels of the Royal Navy also had to intervene on the behalf of British citizens in Japan. Such an incident occurred in September 1862 when Samurai of the Prince of Satsuma killed an Englishman. After repeated attempts to negotiate a satisfactory settlement with the assistance of the Shogun the navy finally sent a squadron under the Commander-in-Chief of the China Station, Rear-Admiral Augustus Kuper, to bombard the port of Kagoshima and force the Prince to pay the full indemnity requested. The bombardment of Kagoshima by the *Argus, Coquette, Euryalus, Havock, Pearl, Perseus* and *Racehorse* was notable for the fact that Armstrong's new breech-loading guns were in action for the first time. The guns, on which the navy had pinned such great hopes, unfortunately proved a dismal failure, twenty-eight accidents occurring to twenty-one guns during the 365 rounds fired. This set the seal of fate on the breech-loader and the navy reverted to the old muzzle-loader for the next 15 years. The British ships suffered considerably from the land based guns and returned to Yokohama where other British warships had arrived from China. Slowly the situation eased and gradually the Shogun fell into disfavour with the British who then lent their support for a return to power by the Mikado, a move welcomed by the Prince of Satsuma.

The incident at Kagoshima was followed by action against the Prince of Nagato, an anti-foreigner who wanted to disrupt external trade. The navy again supported the Shogun, this time forcing the straits of Shimonoseki in September 1864 with the

Conqueror, a ship-of-the-line, and six other French, Dutch and American vessels. This action finally convinced the Prince of Satsuma that he would not be able to defeat the foreigners and the original indemnity demanded for the murder of the merchant was paid in full.

Across the world other gunboats of the navy were keeping peace in the Caribbean. Vessels were sent to put down rebellions in Jamaica and Haiti and to suppress the Fenians in Canada during the middle 1860's. Further small squadrons of gunboats and small vessels were kept hard at work protecting British interests along the west coast of Africa and stamping out the last of the slave traders off the east and west coast of the continent.

By March 1862 the American Civil War was well into its stride with bitter land fighting between the two sides. At sea, however, events had progressed only slowly, the Confederate blockade proving too effective. Means were at hand, though, to try and combat the blockade with a revolutionary vessel that the Union was building. Spies, however, had reported the plans for the new vessel and the Confederates were not slow to take up the challenge. By March 1862 the vessels of both sides were completed and action was joined in the now famous battle between the *Merrimac* and *Monitor*. Tactically neither ship gained the advantage, but strategically the *Monitor* had altered the very nature of naval warfare by the revolutionary carriage of her gun in an armoured revolving turret. The turret protected the gun crew from enemy fire and gave the gun the capability to fire in any direction irrespective of the position or course of the ship.

In Great Britain the battle had a profound effect in certain quarters, as evidenced by a letter to *The Times* which said, "whereas we had available for immediate purposes 149 warships, we now have two, these being the *Warrior* and *Black Prince*. There is not a ship in the English Navy apart from these two that it would not be madness to trust to an engagement with the *Monitor*".

But even the *Warrior* and *Black Prince* had been made obsolete by the *Monitor*. With her revolving armoured turret 8in thick a monitor type vessel could run circles round the British ironclads with their fixed broadside firing guns protected by only 4½in armour plate. Not only the British ironclads were obsolete but also 40 other ironclads completed or under construction in Europe.

Following the completion of the *Warrior* and *Black Prince* a number of smaller vessels were built all making some advance on the design of the two large ironclads. In the same year as the *Monitor* fought the *Merrimac* the *Defence* and *Resistance* were completed. Although much smaller than the *Warrior* (6150 tons as against 9210 tons) they were an improvement in that their whole battery of 16 guns was placed behind the armour belt, which had been extended fore and aft. As an additional weapon they were completed with a ram bow which then became the dictum of naval construction in the Victorian era. The *Defence* and *Resistance* were followed by the *Hector* and *Valiant* and the *Achilles*, a vessel originally planned to have been a sister ship to the *Hector*. Reed, however, had already noted the lack of armour protection to the steering gear of earlier vessels and had it rectified in the *Achilles*, which was enlarged from the 6710 tons of the *Hector* to 9280 tons. The armour belt was extended for the whole length of the waterline and the guns placed behind armour. In addition more powerful engines were fitted, and the sail area as completed was the largest ever set in a warship. So successful did the design of *Achilles* prove that three other similar vessels were designed—the *Agincourt*, *Minotaur* and *Northumberland*.

While these new ironclads were under construction great efforts were made to build up the effective strength of the Royal Navy by converting wooden ships-of-the-line into ironclads. A number of vessels had the upper decks removed and armour plates fitted round the sides. Ships so converted were the *Caledonia* (1860), *Ocean* (1860), *Prince Consort* (1860), *Repulse* (1859), *Royal Alfred* (1859), *Royal Oak* (1860), and *Zealous* (1859). As well as these converted vessels three other ironclads (*Lord Clyde*, *Lord Warden* and *Pallas*) were completed with wooden hulls in an attempt to clear the large stocks of timber stored in the dockyards for the construction of the "wooden walls". However, none of the conversions was very successful and the vessels were soon relegated to minor duties.

Apart from the large number of almost useless wooden vessels in the navy, numerous gunboats left over from the Crimean War were also found to be valueless. Many had been completed towards the end of the war and then placed straight into reserve. As they had been built in a hurry unseasoned timber had had to be used. Although on completion the Admiralty had spent huge sums of money putting the vessels on slips under wooden sheds the unpreserved timber had over the years deteriorated and fallen apart with dry rot. In addition to the poor timber, the engines of these gunboats were of an early design and rapidly wore out. The effective strength of the navy in small vessels was thus greatly reduced. The conception of the gunboat had been proved during the Crimean War and in 1864 the Admiralty tried to extend this idea to larger warships, building three armoured gunboats, the *Viper*, *Vixen* and *Waterwitch*, armed with two 7in MLR. The vessels proved a failure in service, even the *Waterwitch* which had been fitted with a revolutionary turbine for propulsion being unsatisfactory. However, the construction of small gunboats continued, each new class incorporating some innovations. The one main advance occurred in 1867 when the *Plover* class, armed with a 7in MLR and two 64-pdrs was fitted with two small screws, due to the very shallow draught required, precluding the use of a single large screw. Twin screws were not looked upon with favour, the idea being accepted mainly because of the requirements of the ship's design.

In the meantime the action between the *Monitor* and *Merrimac* had aroused the interest of a Captain Cowper Phipps Coles who redesigned an idea he had first formulated during the Crimean War. While on service in the Black Sea he had built the *Lady Nancy*, a small gunboat of shallow draught on which he had mounted a 32-pdr gun in a shield. Following up this idea Captain Coles patented a plan in 1860 for a turret sunk into an armoured breastwork and then put forward plans to the Admiralty for a ship mounting ten of his turrets each with two guns, and revolving on a series of rollers. After studying the plans the Admiralty ordered an experimental turret which was tested on board the *Trusty* at Shoeburyness. Captain Coles finally managed to persuade the Admiralty to accept his idea in February 1862 and he at once set about having the *Prince Albert* constructed. This ship, the Royal Navy's first iron turret ship was finally completed with four turrets in 1866, but, in the meantime Captain Coles had worked upon his ideas, and the Admiralty, and converted the steam ship-of-the-line *Royal Sovereign* into a turret ironclad. She was one of the last of the old wooden ship-of-the-line vessels, carrying 131 guns in the conventional broadside on her three decks. The top two decks were removed and with the weight thus saved she was fitted with four of Captain Coles' turrets and her sides covered with 4½in armour. The forward turret carried two and the other three turrets single 12½-ton guns and they were all turned by hand. The conversion was completed in 1864.

While Captain Coles was busy developing his ideas for turret ships, Reed, with one of his assistants, had developed a new method for constructing the hull of a warship. Known as the longitudinal bracket frame system, it became the standard method of construction up to the end of the century.

The first warship completed with the new method of construction was the *Bellerophon*, launched in May 1865. A number of other innovations were also built into the vessel. To increase manoeuverability and speed the length of the vessel was short compared with the *Warrior*, and attempts were made at increasing the fighting capability by carrying a small armoured battery in the bows, thus developing end-on fire without any sacrifice to the weight of broadside that could be delivered. This was not entirely successful, as it hampered movement at sea. Reed was convinced that only *high*-sided vessels gained full stability, especially when they were fully rigged, as was the *Bellerophon*. The citadel protected all the vital parts of the ship, such as the engines and guns, and the armoured belt extended for the whole length of the waterline. In addition she was the first vessel to be completed with a double bottom for the whole of her length (the *Warrior* having a double bottom under the engine spaces only) giving far greater protection against underwater damage. A balanced rudder was a further improvement that was built into the design of the *Bellerophon*, and again she was the first ship to be so fitted. This greatly facilitated the handling of the vessel and helped towards reducing her turning circle.

The *Hercules* was the next vessel to be completed, in 1868, and she was just an enlarged version of the *Bellerophon*. At the same time as these vessels were under construction the *Penelope*, a vessel designed for river service with a shallow draught was completed with twin screws.

During 1865 Captain Coles presented the Admiralty with

further plans which they recast and ordered as the *Monarch*. Captain Coles was not at all pleased with the alterations made to his plans. As redrawn the vessel was provided with a fo'c'sle and poop, which deprived her of end-on fire, although this was to some extent compensated for by the siting of two 6½-ton guns in armoured positions in the fo'c'sle. Reed was also unhappy with the plans for the *Monarch*, but for different reasons. He was to say of the *Monarch*, "No satisfactorily designed turret ship with rigging has yet been built". This statement was to have a tragic confirmation in 1870. In the Admiralty's view the fo'c'sle was necessary for seaworthiness, but Captain Coles so complained of the *Monarch* that the Admiralty gave him *carte blanche* to design another turret ship incorporating his own ideas. Lairds, the shipbuilding firm of Birkenhead, were contracted to build the new vessel—the *Captain*—as they had had most experience in producing turret ships (such as the *Scorpion* and *Wivern*). In effect the *Captain* turned out to be an enlarged *Monarch*, magnifying all the faults of that vessel. The one main difference lay in the decks, the *Captain* having only two as against the three of the *Monarch*. Another recognisable feature was the masts, which in the *Captain* were tripods as opposed to the single pole in the *Monarch*. Protection for the fo'c'sle in the *Captain* was dispensed with and the whole structure much enlarged, so as to keep the ship dry when steaming against a head sea. When she was launched it was found that the *Captain* floated with a freeboard that was two feet lower than that for which she had been designed.

Reed was highly critical, both of the *Monarch* and especially of the *Captain*. Captain Coles, however, gathered a large following in his struggle against the gradual evolution of Reed's ideas, sending many letters to the National Press in support of his campaign for turret ships. Captain Coles was convinced that his idea for turning a tun in a turret was better than turning the ship to fire the guns. However, Captain Coles also believed that for the guns to be effective the ship should have *low* sides, which reduced the righting moment of the vessel, and that in addition to the engines, the ship should be fully rigged. Referring to his new plans for the *Captain* he wrote to *The Times* of April 1862 saying, "I will undertake to prove that on my principle a vessel shall be built nearly 100 feet shorter than the *Warrior*, and in all

D

respects equal to her, with one exception, that I will undertake to disable and capture her within one hour".

The late 1860's not only witnessed a revolution in warship design but also amongst the men. Promotion and length of service had long been a bone of contention and during the decade the system of recruitment for the lower deck was revised. This had to come. By 1870 the ships had become so complex with such highly technical equipment that the old methods of recruitment and training were no longer applicable. No longer was a seaman a "Jack of all trades" able to turn a hand to any work on board. Many new branches were formed as a result of the technological advancements, not the least among these being in the engineering and gunnery fields. Promotion for officers had also much improved since Queen Victoria's Order in Council of 1840, which forcibly retired a number of captains from the service. This was further improved in 1869 when the regulations limited the number of nominations a flag officer could put forward for the selection of midshipmen. This reduced the patronage allowed a flag officer to three, a commodore two, and captains of seagoing ships one, with no officer being allowed to put forward a second candidate within the space of three years.

At the same time, in the Spring Estimates of 1869, Hugh Childers, the First Lord was forced under the direction of Mr. Gladstone's Liberal Government to reduce expenditure. In so doing he reduced the number of men serving on foreign stations from 17,000 to 11,000 in spite of the protests of the First Sea Lord, Sir Alexander Milne. To accomplish this, the larger and more stable colonies such as Canada, Australia and New Zealand were requested to provide certain forces for their own defence.

Not only conditions and ships improved during the 1860's but great advances were also made in the field of gunnery. Armstrong had developed his idea for a rifle-bored breech-loading gun. With the increased accuracy, range and penetration achieved by the weapon the Admiralty was forced to increase the thickness of armour plate fitted to warships. With the need for increase in the thickness of armour plate, the displacement increased to such an extent that it became impracticable to protect a ship over its whole length, and so it was decided to place the protection over the most vital parts of the warship—the engines, gun turrets and magazines. This formed a central armoured citadel around which was built the hull of the vessel. To be effective this meant that the guns had to be centred amidships in turrets, and so the broadside disappeared from fighting ships. As armour protection advanced, problems were encountered with the new gun designs. Armstrong's gun failed to achieve its expectations and, as related earlier, had to be removed from service. This left the navy without a reliable gun for its warships, and so, as a matter of expediency it was decided to revert to the old muzzle-loading type of gun. In 1865 the Royal Gun Factories produced a new type of muzzle-loader for testing which proved satisfactory. Basically it was built on the same principle as Armstrong's gun by shrinking tubes onto one another, the inner tube being rifled. Although the muzzle-loader took much longer to prepare for firing compared to the breech-loader, it did provide the navy with a reliable weapon until the breech-loader could be sufficiently well developed.

CHAPTER 7

The Battleship Develops

*The fashion in ships of war is as fickle as that of
ladies' hats*

GLADSTONE

IN SEPTEMBER 1870 the Royal Navy suffered a disaster which
shook the service to the core of its foundation. During the night
of September 6th the *Captain* in company with the Channel
Fleet consisting of the *Agincourt, Bellerophon, Bristol, Hercules,
Inconstant, Lord Warden, Minotaur, Monarch* and *Northumberland*
forced her way through the teeth of a gale raging in the Bay of
Biscay. Admiral Sir Alexander Milne, C-in-C of the Mediterranean Fleet, who spent some time on board the *Captain* during
the day remarked on what appeared to him to be a dangerous
roll. The *Captain* at the time was heeling 12 to 14 degrees.
During the night the squadron became dispersed and at daylight
on the 7th, when it again came together, it was found that the
Captain was missing. Of her crew of 500 only 18 survived to
reach land, Captain Hugh Burgoyne VC, the commanding
officer, and Captain Cowper Phipps Coles, her designer, going
down with the ship.

A court martial was at once convened to enquire into the
cause of the loss of the *Captain.* It was a particularly delicate
enquiry to conduct in view of the previous friction between
Captain Coles and Reed, the Controller of the navy Sir Spencer
Robinson, and the First Lord of the Admiralty Hugh Childers,
who lost his only son when the *Captain* went down.

After much discussion and heartfelt searching the court finally
noted that the *Captain* did not possess the "required amount of
stability", due in fact to her very low freeboard and heavy sails
and masts, matters which gave rise to a high centre of gravity.
On the night of the accident the ship was rolling heavily, and a

sudden extra strong gust of wind striking the double-reefed top-sails and fore-topmost staysail coupled with a broadside wave hitting the ship along her keel line at the height of a roll, pushed the vessel past her point of no return. At the end of the report the members of the court martial concluded that, "the *Captain* was built in deference to public opinion expressed in Parliament and through other channels and in opposition to the views and opinions of the Controller of the Navy and his Department".

In fact Reed's assistant, Nathaniel Barnaby, who took over as President of the Council of Construction in July 1870, when Reed resigned as Chief Constructor, had conducted a number of experiments on the question of stability in 1867. These had been ordered, when it was proposed to cut down a number of two-deck ships, arm them with turrets, and give them masts. Even at that time Barnaby calculated theoretically, that if the edge of the deck on a low-sided ship should reach the level of the sea, she would be in a dangerous position. He calculated that if the vessel continued to heel past this point, then the position of maximum stability would soon be reached, and would then be dramatically reduced as the righting force of the vessel was diminished. This was only a theory, however, and it took the capsizing of the *Captain* to prove the dangerous significance of a low-sided vessel equipped with a heavy weight of masts and turrets on an upper deck, giving rise to a high centre of gravity.

The loss of the *Captain* had further repercussions in the Admiralty. Reed had already resigned as Chief Constructor when his adverse views of the *Captain* came into conflict with those of Captain Coles and the First Lord. Having lost his only son in the *Captain*, Childers felt that the Controllers Department was to some extent to blame for the loss of the vessel, and as Reed had resigned, he transferred his adverse feelings to the Controller, Sir Spencer Robinson. The feud between the two men grew with the passage of time. Then the First Lord produced a minute on the loss of the *Captain*, in which he put the responsibility for the loss on the Controller, and Reed, both of whom had opposed the design. Finally in February 1871 Sir Spencer Robinson was forced to resign his post following an interview with the Prime Minister, Mr. W. E. Gladstone. The First Lord himself was then forced to resign his post a month later following an illness, and he was succeeded by Mr. G. J. Goschen.

The loss of the *Captain* created much apprehension about turret ships and was indeed tragic, but it was not calamitous and the court martial clearly showed up the defects in her design. Steps, however, had already been taken before the disaster to remedy one of the gravest errors. The Admiralty had realised that steam and sail would not mix, and that to install both systems in the new generation of warships seriously impaired the fighting efficiency of a vessel, and would be courting disaster. As a result of the *Captain*'s loss the turret ship *Monarch* was subjected to many exhaustive tests which proved the vessel to be entirely satisfactory.

In the same month as the *Captain* capsized two new ironclads, the *Audacious* and *Vanguard*, were completed. Together with the *Invincible* and *Iron Duke* they formed a class of six ships. Designed by Reed they proved to have the steadiest gun platform of any vessel in the fleet, being excellent seaboats, and developing axial fire from their main armament of ten 9in MLR guns in any weather. They were, however, completed without any wing bulkheads, which in the case of the *Vanguard* proved a disaster. The last two vessels to be completed, the *Swiftsure* and *Triumph* (which were single screw vessels as opposed to the rest of the class which were twin screw) were the subject of an experiment by the Admiralty to re-introduce copper-sheathing to the hulls of warships. This had been done with the old "wooden-walls" to prevent the hulls from rotting due to marine growth and attack from the teredo worm. It was found with the new ironclads, that although the hull was impervious to the teredo worm, it was far more prone to fouling, the growths appearing more quickly than on the old wooden vessels. The experiment was a success, only a slight loss in speed being sustained, although in the case of the *Swiftsure* the tonnage was increased by almost 900 tons.

In 1873 a new vessel appeared in the Navy Lists. Named the *Devastation* she was totally different in one respect from any previous warship in the navy, and embodied a number of alterations to her design suggested by a Special Committee of Designs. Masts and associated rigging were dispensed with in the new vessel, her guns being given the ability to fire in any direction. The turrets carrying the guns were sited high up amidships fore and aft, and were also different from those of other turret ships, being in an armoured casemate which pivoted, allowing the gun to aim in any direction. Her sister ship *Thunderer* wasn't finally completed until 1877 when she emerged with one of her turrets mounting 12·5in guns instead of the 12in of the *Devastation*. A third sister ship, the *Fury*, also came in for criticism from the Special Committee on Designs. She had been laid down in September 1870, but after the Committee's report, construction ceased in 1871. By that time she had been completed up to the armoured main deck. The plans were redrawn by Barnaby's secretary, Mr. W. H. White, and she was finally completed in 1879 as the *Dreadnought*. As such she was the last true ironclad completed for the navy and had a freeboard of uniform height throughout her length. In addition she was completed without portholes in her sides, fresh air being provided by forced ventilation, the first ship to be so fitted. Apart from this there were one or two other notable features about the *Dreadnought*. She was the first ship to be completed with a longitudinal bulkhead amidships and also among the first to be fitted with the new compound engines. Machinery had made many advances since it was first introduced into the navy. Compared to the first ironclad *Warrior* the compound vertical triple expansion engines of the *Dreadnought* developed 8210HP on a displacement of 10,460 tons to give her a speed of 14 knots. The *Warrior* had developed 5270HP with her horizontal trunk single expansion engine giving her a speed of 14 knots on a displacement of 9210 tons.

In 1871 the Admiralty had formed the Special Committee on Designs whose purpose was to draw up reports on all the designs then under construction in the Admiralty, and to make recommendations for the future lines of development. The Committee made a close study of the current designs and stated that, "as powerful armament, thick armour, speed, and light draught cannot be combined in one ship, although all are needed for the defence of the country; there is no alternative but to give preponderance to each in its turn amongst different classes of ships which shall mutually supplement one another". As a result of the report, differing designs were produced concentrating on one of these aspects, and led directly to the development of the scouting cruiser, battlecruiser and battleship concept, of a completely defensible offensive fleet.

Another of the suggestions put forward by the Committee was that the armoured central citadel on warships should be greatly shortened, a practice followed in the Italian *Caio Duilio*. Already the Committee had made certain suggestions regarding the plans for the *Devastation*, and they then turned their attention to the *Inflexible*. By 1874 the plans for this new vessel were completed. Previous adverse comment in the press and Parliament regarding vessels with low hatchway freeboards fore and aft, such as the *Captain*, had very much influenced the design of the upperworks on the *Inflexible*. As a result she was planned with a high hatchway freeboard along her whole length, forcing the designers to place her two turrets in echelon. The guns themselves were also new, weighing 100 tons each, the heaviest guns in the navy, but they were still of the old muzzle loading type. The barrels of the new guns were very long, much longer than the diameter of the turret which housed them, which meant that they had to be loaded from outside the turret, and behind a specially constructed glacis. In addition to these innovations the *Inflexible* was equipped with two of the new torpedo tubes in submerged positions. With all the alterations and new equipment the *Inflexible* wasn't finally completed until 1881.

By the 1870's the ram bow had become a notable feature of many warships and the *Sultan*, the successor to the *Hercules*, developed the theory of end-on fire to combat the new menace. Instead of the one small gun of the *Hercules*, the *Sultan* mounted four 12½-ton MLR guns capable of ahead firing. For her main armament she mounted eight 18-ton MLR guns. As such she was the last central battery ironclad to have been designed by Reed before he resigned from office.

The idea of the ram had gained such ascendancy in certain quarters of the Admiralty that plans were drawn up for a ship specially designed for ramming. Although responsible for laying down this ship, the *Hotspur*, in 1868, Reed had very little faith in her. She did not even carry her 25-ton MLR gun in a turret when completed. Instead it was placed in a fixed armoured citadel and was manoeuvred into one of several ports placed in the structure. This was later replaced by a turret mounting two 25-ton MLR guns.

Having completed designing the *Hotspur*, which he at once dismissed from his mind, Reed set about designing a new class of four-coast defence battleships, called *Cyclops*, *Gorgon*, *Hecate* and *Hydra*, which were known as breastwork type monitors. This class was followed by another similar type of vessel, the *Glatton*, which had the dubious distinction of having the lowest freeboard of any ship in the navy, just three feet! She had a single turret and an armour belt 12 inches thick and when joining action her reserve coal bunkers, which never carried coal, were flooded for ballast to lower the silhouette of the ship. She proved to be the ultimate in coast defence ship design for the Royal Navy. She was followed by a rather inferior ram vessel, the *Rupert*, which was the last vessel of this type to be built. Basically the *Rupert* was an enlarged *Hotspur* with a single turret forward carrying two 18-ton MLR and two 64-pdr MLR guns aft in a fixed breastwork.

One of the more unusual designs produced during the 1870's was based upon the influence of the ram and a new weapon, the torpedo. This vessel, the *Polyphemus*, was designed in 1873 by Barnaby at the request of certain officers. Barnaby was not in favour with the ideas he was forced to incorporate into the design, and the vessel proved a dismal failure. Her main innovation was the new torpedo tubes, about which Barnaby had strong reservations. Originally the torpedo had been invented by a Mr. Whitehead in 1866. In essence it was a long tube, the major part of which held the propulsion unit driven by compressed air. Its offensive capability was in the form of an explosive charge placed in the nose of the weapon and fired by a pistol which was actuated on contact with a hard object. Whitehead built and tested the first weapons at Fiume, which then formed part of the Austro-Hungarian Empire. The Admiralty were offered the exclusive rights to the weapon, but they turned them down on the grounds that the torpedo would threaten Britain's naval supremacy. Limited rights on the weapon were sold to Austria, whereon the Admiralty altered its views and bought the manufacturing rights in 1871. Soon a tube was developed to fire the new torpedo and its range had increased to just over 100 yards. By 1873 it had developed sufficiently to make it a weapon suitable for use on board a warship and so the *Polyphemus* was designed to carry five of the new tubes for the torpedo, in submerged positions, one in the bow and four broad-side. In addition the *Polyphemus* was given an armament of six 6-pdr guns with which to repel any small boat that was armed with torpedoes.

Towards the end of 1875 a new type of vessel was launched. Developed from ideas put forward by Barnaby, and put into practise in the *Inconstant*, a high speed heavily armed cruiser without armour protection, the new vessel was named the *Shannon*. The *Shannon* was the first armoured cruiser in the Royal Navy, and went some way towards carrying out the proposals suggested by the Special Committee on Designs. Barnaby himself felt that the best means of defence was to attack, and in carrying out this concept he concentrated more on the armament of ships than on the armour, as opposed to Reed who had built vessels that were heavily armoured as well as being heavily gunned. In the *Shannon*, Barnaby sacrificed protection in favour of the heavier armament. She did have an armour belt, but it was only 9 inches at its thickest part, and extended for only three-quarters of the waterline. Instead of the complete armour belt, the *Shannon* was given an armoured deck and her hull well subdivided, the forward subdivisions, where there was no pro-tective belt, being filled with the coal supply. The armament comprised two ahead firing 10in MLR placed in embrasures, and six broadside firing 9in MLR and one stern firing 9in MLR.

Although the basic idea for the *Shannon* proved successful the vessel herself was a failure. She was completed as a fully-rigged ship, the last British armoured warship to be completed with sails, and was propelled by a single screw. The compound horizontal engines gave inferior results and could only develop 3370HP, to give the vessel a speed of 12 knots. The Admiralty were convinced that although the *Shannon* herself was a failure further ships should be constructed with their plans based upon the same ideas. As a result the *Nelson* and *Northampton* were constructed, but they too unfortunately inherited the same faults as the *Shannon*. Barnaby was also convinced of the practicability of the basic design stating, "they may be looked upon as armoured ships having to meet armoured ships—or, as protected cruisers . . .". The Controller of the navy, Rear-Admiral Houstan Stewart, held different views of those to Barnaby as to the purpose for which ships of this type should be constructed.

He felt that, "their object was not to take part in a close engagement but to roam over the seas and drive away unarmoured fast cruisers from harrying our commerce".

During the decade a new naval force began to emerge which in forty years' time was to sorely test the strength and capabilities of the Royal Navy. A unified Germany led by Chancellor Bismarck had commenced building a navy, the nucleus of which had been formed after the Crimean War when Britain had given Germany a frigate and a gunboat. The High Seas Fleet developed rapidly, and by 1872 two naval bases were in operation, at Kiel and Wilhelmshaven. In spite of this development, and in the prevailing political climate, Great Britain still looked upon France as posing her greatest threat to peace.

Early in 1872 the navy fitted out an expedition under the command of Captain George Nares in command of the wooden steam corvette *Challenger*, to carry out research in the Atlantic, Pacific and Antarctic oceans. Sailing in 1872 the expedition remained away for three and a half years covering a distance of almost 70,000 miles. On board the *Challenger* was a team of three naturalists, a chemist, a geologist and a photographer under the leadership of Professor Wyville Thompson. The purpose of the expedition was to take soundings and record sea temperatures and to take samples of the ocean bed for animal life. In addition the chemist was to analyse any mineral content of the salt water. A certain amount of coastal surveying work was also undertaken and a number of magnetic observations made. The *Challenger* finally returned to England in May 1876 when the results were processed and published in fifteen volumes.

In September 1875 the Royal Navy suffered a second setback. Although not so tragic as the loss of the *Captain*, this second accident gave rise to much thought concerning the design of the navy's warships. The accident occurred in fog off Kingston in the Irish Channel, while the reserve squadron of the Channel Fleet was exercising. At 12.50 on September 1st the broadside ironclad ram *Iron Duke* rammed her sister ship the *Vanguard* amidships on the port side. The ram pierced the engine room of the *Vanguard* which soon sank, although prompt rescue operations ensured that no lives were lost. The court martial found that the main reasons for the accident arose from human error. These were the high speed of the squadron in poor visibility, the commander of the said division of ships leaving the deck of his ship before the manoeuvre in process of evolution was completed, unnecessary reduction of speed by the *Vanguard* without being ordered to do so, and without signalling such a move to the *Iron Duke*, increase of speed by the *Iron Duke* and by the said ship improperly shearing out of line, and for not making fog signals.

Apart from these human errors the court also concluded that the *Vanguard* foundered as a result of being holed in the most vital transverse bulkhead, between the engine and boiler rooms, the inrush of water extinguishing the boilers, and finding its way through improperly closed watertight doors to the provision hold. Finally the whole blame for the loss of the vessel was placed upon its captain, his second-in-command and the navigating officer, all of whom were severely reprimanded.

The accident immediately focused attentions on the ram bow, with which many warships were fitted, for it was found on inspection that the *Iron Duke*'s ram bow had suffered no damage at all. Amongst the many ram vessels completed for the navy were the *Amethyst* class corvettes completed between 1873 and 1875. These proved to be the last wooden warships to be built for the navy.

The *Amethyst* herself was involved in an incident with the Peruvian navy in 1877. During a revolution in May 1877 the British built armoured turret ship *Huascar*, the flagship of the Peruvian navy, was taken over by rebels. Under the rebels the *Huascar* stopped a number of British merchant ships seizing their coal. The British Government was then forced to intervene in the matter and sent the *Shah*, flagship of the Pacific Station, to intercept the *Huascar*. Together with the *Amethyst* the *Shah* intercepted the Peruvian ship on May 29th, Admiral De Horsey demanding surrender of the *Huascar*, which was refused. Fire was opened at 15.00, the upperworks of the *Huascar* suffering considerable damage from about 60 hits, half of which had been fired by the *Amethyst*. The armour of the rebel ship proved impervious to the British shellfire, and after about two hours the *Shah* fired a torpedo, which failed to reach the target. The fight reached an inconclusive end and during the night the *Huascar* sailed away and surrendered to the Peruvian forces. Had she stayed to fight the outcome might have been different, for after dark Admiral De Horsey launched a steam pinnace armed with another torpedo. The action was also notable for it was the last time a wooden warship of the Royal Navy was in action armed with a broadside battery of muzzle loading guns.

The *Huascar* incident proved to be just a passing scare. Of far more importance to the Admiralty was the relations with Russia during 1877 and 1878. Relations deteriorated to such an extent during the time that the Russo-Turkish war was in progress that the Admiralty fully expected that war would be declared, and in anticipation of such an event purchased four battleships that were under construction in England for foreign powers. One of these vessels was completing for Brazil and the other three for Turkey, Great Britain being forced to detain these under conditions of neutrality. The Brazilian vessel had been designed by Reed, and was an improved *Monarch* type of vessel. On commissioning for the navy she was renamed *Neptune*. Her main claim to fame was that she was the first British warship to be completed with a bathroom.

The Turkish vessels were never successful, one being an improved *Hercules* type of ship and being renamed *Superb*, the other two being sister ships and renamed *Belleisle* and *Orion*. The design of these last two was similar to existing coast defence ships but they were smaller than the *Hotspur*.

All four vessels were obsolete when purchased, their designs having long been superseded by newer ideas, already in service in the Royal Navy.

By 1877 the torpedo was being fitted in a number of warships of the navy, and in that same year was used in action by the *Shah*. Realising its potential the commanding officer of the gunnery school *Excellent* formed a new branch in 1872 which taught the mechanics of torpedo warfare to the new generation of officers. In charge of the gunnery school at that time was a certain Captain J. A. Fisher who did all in his power to foster the new weapon. In the year that the torpedo school moved to a new base at HMS *Vernon*, Captain Fisher left the *Excellent*, having done as he put it, "my utmost to develop it, from a conviction that the issue of the next naval war will chiefly depend on the use that is made of the torpedo, not only in ocean warfare, but for the purposes of blockade". How true a prophecy this was to be was not realised until 1917.

In the same year that the *Shah* fought the *Huascar*, 1877, the yard of Thornycroft completed a vessel specially built to carry and launch a new weapon. With a speed of $18\frac{1}{2}$ knots she was commissioned as the *Lightning*, the Royal Navy's first torpedo boat. Two further torpedo boats under construction for Russia by Yarrow were purchased in 1877, when the Russo-Turkish war broke out. They were both present at the naval review in the Solent the following year.

In 1878 yet another type of vessel entered the Navy Lists. This was the *Comus* class of eleven ships rated as protected cruisers. Their displacement was only 2380 tons and they carried two 6-ton MLR and twelve 64-pdr guns. In service they attained speeds of up to 13 knots and were completed between 1878 and 1884. Again the design was based on the conception of the *Shannon* although with these cruisers the only protection was a $1\frac{1}{2}$ inch thick deck sited amidships over the engine room. One great advance was made with the *Comus* class, which was to have a profound effect on future warship construction, as will be related in Volume Two of this history. During the 1870's a number of experiments had been conducted, both in this country and abroad, with a view to improving the quality of the iron used in ships' boilers. These had, for some time, been giving trouble, and it was felt that the cracks that were appearing in the boiler tubes were probably caused by inferior quality iron used during the construction. As a result of the experiments a new process was evolved for purifying the iron and the new material produced, namely steel, was found to be much stronger and durable than iron. As a result the Admiralty specified that the *Comus* class should be constructed entirely of the new material and they were the first all-steel ships completed for the Royal Navy.

There was one other unsuccessful design produced by the Royal Navy during the 1870's and that was the *Temeraire*. A brig-rigged ship she was designed to carry the heaviest guns ever built. These were four 11in and for the first time in the navy these were placed in a barbette and not in a turret. In many ways the design itself was completely successful but was a complete failure economically, no more ships of the type being built.

Although far from complete the *Inflexible* design appeared so good that more ships of her type were ordered by the Admiralty. As a result the *Agamemnon* and *Ajax* were laid down in 1876 and launched in 1879–1880. They were smaller versions of the *Inflexible* and not nearly so powerful. When completed they were the last warships in the navy to carry muzzle-loading guns and were the first battleships to carry a definite secondary armament.

Apart from the gradual evolution of the ships, conditions for the men continued to improve during the 1870's as well. At the beginning of the decade the last of the old officers left over from the previous wars were officially retired when the Navy List split the headings of commissioned officers into Active and Retired. At long last the way for promotion was clear, the whole process having taken from 1847 to 1870 to achieve. Apart from better promotion prospects the man entering the navy had many different branches for which he could be selected, according to his talents. This applied not only to ordinary seamen but to officers as well. By the end of the 1870's branches had been formed covering torpedoes, gunnery, signals, navigation, engineering etc. and all had commissioned officers appointed by Commission of the Admiralty, in addition to the warrant officers appointed by Warrant of the Navy board. Even former civilian posts were now given to commissioned officers, viz: Paymasters (formerly Pursers), Surgeons, Chaplains, and Naval Instructors (formerly Schoolmasters). These were given the full status of branches in 1864 (except Chaplains). The highest rank attainable by these many branches was then the rank of Captain, but even this was to change in time.

Credits for Illustrations

Author's Collection: 128 (upper)

Imperial War Museum: 65, 70 (left), 75 (lower), 77, 80 (upper), 82 (upper), 90 (upper), 100, 102 (upper), 131 (lower), 132 (upper), 133, 141, 142, 143 (upper)

Mansell Collection: 66 (lower), 67, 68 (upper), 69 (lower), 70 (right), 71 (upper), 72, 73, 74, 75 (upper), 76 (upper), 78, 79, 80 (lower two), 81 (upper), 82 (lower right), 84, 86 (upper), 89 (upper), 90 (lower), 91 (upper), 92, 93, 94 (upper), 95 (upper), 98 (lower), 103, 104 (upper), 105, 107, 108, 115, 120 (lower), 123, 125, 127, 128 (lower), 129, 130, 136/137, 144

Tom Molland: 121 (lower)

Radio Times Hulton Picture Library: 66 (upper), 68 (lower), 69 (upper), 71 (lower), 76 (lower), 82 (lower left), 83, 85 (upper), 86 (lower), 87, 88, 89 (lower), 91 (lower), 94 (lower), 95 (lower), 96, 97, 98 (upper), 99, 101, 106 (upper), 112 (upper), 113 (upper), 118, 119, 120, (toptwo), 135, 138, 139, 140, 143 (uqqer)

Real Photographs: 109 (foot), 116 (lower)

P.A. Vicary: 81 (lower), 85 (lower), 102 (lower), 104 (lower), 106 (lower), 109 (top and centre), 110, 111, 112 (lower), 113 (lower), 114, 116 (upper), 117, 121 (upper), 122, 124, 126, 131 (upper), 132 (lower), 134, 143 (lower)

*At the end of the Napoleonic wars the main
power of the Royal Navy remained the
sailing ship-of-the-line.   The development
of warships had been so slow that ships like
the one above were virtually the same as at
the start of the eighteenth century and were
to remain so for another sixty years.*

E

*Although the lot of the sailor
was a hard one, there were
moments when he could relax
and enjoy himself, usually in
harbour.*

*The press-gang remained the
standard method of "recruiting"
the crews of ships right up to
the 1830s. The favourite
victims were sailors of
merchant ships returning home
from abroad. Nobody,
however, was immune from the
gang, the waterman right
being seized at Tower Hill on
his wedding day.*

Anyone who put up resistance to the press-gang was forcibly taken and put in prison. The following day he would be handcuffed and marched under strong escort to the ship.

The Point of Honor.

ABOVE LEFT: *Flogging was a common sight on board a warship. The "cat" had a wooden handle 18in long, to which was bound nine 28in long thongs of heavy duty cord, each cord having two knots tied in it. The "cat" was always kept in a red or green baize bag, and after use was always thrown overboard. The articles of war stated that every man on board had to watch the sentence being carried out, which on occasions had been 100 lashes, only rarely the death sentence of 1000 lashes being ordered. Officially officers were immune to the sentence, which could only be ordered by the captain of the ship.*

BELOW LEFT: *Another of the punishments endured by the sailor was starting. This could be inflicted by the bosun at will, and was usually applied to a sailor who was lazy, or a bit slow in replying to an order. It was administered by a thick piece of rope with a knot in it, and the man was beaten about the body for as long as thought necessary.*

TOP: *Continual flogging, and the drinking of neat rum drove many men mad. In fact there were so many insane at the turn of the century, that the navy had its own lunatic asylum—the Bethlehem Royal Hospital, more commonly called Bedlam. Today this old hospital is the home of the Imperial War Museum.*

RIGHT: *The poor inmates of Bedlam were a continual source of ridicule to the general public, who were allowed into the hospital to view them. A committee in the House of Commons in 1815 condemned the hospital and its medical treatment of patients as antiquated.*

Handling heavy canvas sails, even in calm weather, was no easy job. On the yards the men stood on ropes called ratlines, using both hands to work the canvas. This was often the cause of ruptures, but even as late as 1890 training in the handling of sails was being given aboard the frigate Raleigh.

On August 27th, 1816 Admiral Edward Pellew, in command of a combined British and Dutch squadron, anchored off the African port of Algiers. For many years the Barbary pirates had troubled shipping in the area and Admiral Pellew had orders to destroy the pirates' lair.

ABOVE: *Flying his flag in the* Queen Charlotte (*100-guns*) *Admiral Pellew anchored off the port and requested the Dey to release the hundreds of Europeans held in slavery. The Dey refused and fire was opened.*

BELOW: *Three broadsides were fired at Algiers and the following day the Dey, Omar Pasha, surrendered, paying the indemnity requested and releasing all the Europeans.*

ABOVE LEFT: *The nineteenth century was notable for the large number of explorations and surveys undertaken by the navy. The first of the expeditions was led by Commander John Ross, who left England in 1818 in an attempt to find a North West Passage. For his work in polar exploration John Ross was knighted and rose to the rank of Admiral before he died in 1856. The illustration shows him in later life.*

ABOVE CENTRE: *Another naval officer who spent much of his life exploring was John Franklin. He also was knighted for his* work and rose to the rank of captain, and *would undoubtedly have risen higher had he not met a tragic end on one of his polar explorations. In 1836 he was appointed Governor of Tasmania and sailed on a further polar expedition in 1845. This was the last that was ever seen of John Franklin.*

ABOVE RIGHT: *Following the 1818 expeditions further parties set forth the following year. One of these was fitted out under William Parry who penetrated well into the Arctic Circle in a second attempt to force a North-West passage.*

*In his quest to force a North-West Passage,
Parry sailed through Barrows Strait and
into Melville Sound passing over the
magnetic pole. He was then forced to take
to the sledge, to travel overland before
reaching the Bering Straits.*

LEFT: *John Franklin's command as a
lieutenant was the* Trent. *In her he sailed
in an attempt to reach the North Pole in
the 1818 expedition. Although only a fifth
rate the small* Trent *managed to force her
way through dangerous areas of ice floes in
the 1818 expedition.*

LEFT: *In 1824 Parry tried again to force a way through the ice, and this time was forced to abandon the* Fury *when she became severely damaged by ice. She was the first ship lost by Parry on one of these expeditions.*

RIGHT: *The First Lord of the Admiralty in 1821 was Viscount Melville, Robert Saunders-Dundas. Entirely against his own convictions he ordered the first steam vessel operated by the navy, the paddle tug* Monkey. *In principle he was entirely opposed to steam, and during his term of office little was done to further the use of steam in the navy.*

RIGHT: *The paddle tug* Monkey *was the first steam vessel in the navy. The tug* Bee *shown here was typical of the steam tugs that were operated by the navy and which remained in service for many years.*

In 1827 Captain Sir John Ross
proposed to the Admiralty that a steam
vessel should be used on the next polar
expedition. His idea was turned down, but
he went ahead privately with the plan, and
fitted out the paddle-steamer Victory,
which sailed from Woolwich on May 23rd,
1829.

On October 27th, 1827 a combined British,
French and Russian Squadron, under
Admiral Sir Edward Codrington RN,
annihilated a Turkish squadron at the
Battle of Navarino.

The flagship of Codrington was the Asia, *a second rate of 1824 that remained in the Royal Navy until 1908, when she was sold.*

This was the last time that a battle was fought between sailing ships-of-the-line. True to tradition the Asia laid herself alongside the Turkish flagship of the Captain Bey.

The battle was an overwhelming victory for the Allies, many of the Turkish vessels blowing up when set on fire by fireships.

TOP: *In 1830 the navy formed a technical school for gunnery under Commander Smith. It was not until 1859 that a permanent base for the school was set up on board the old sailing ship* Queen Charlotte. *The* Queen Charlotte, *which had been flagship of Admiral Pellew at Algiers in 1816, was renamed* Excellent *when commissioned for her new duties. The photograph above shows the vessel in her new guise in 1888.*

ABOVE: *In 1830 Lord Melville was replaced as First Lord of the Admiralty by Sir James Graham. Sir James was a great advocate of steam and during his term of*

office did all he could to further its use in the Royal Navy. He had, however, to face great opposition with his revolutionary ideas.

ABOVE: *At the same time as Sir James Graham was appointed First Lord, a new First Sea Lord was appointed. The new man was none other than Nelson's old captain, Sir Thomas Masterman Hardy. He too was a great supporter of steam, but unfortunately his term of office was a short one. The illustration shows him as Vice-Admiral of the Blue and Governor of Greenwich Hospital.*

TOP: *As part of the "new" navy that he planned, Hardy laid down a number of 50-gun frigates, and so successful was the design and conception of these vessels that as late as 1850 such ships were still being laid down in the dockyards. One such vessel was the* Nankin *launched in March 1850.*

ABOVE: *The 46-gun frigates that Lord Melville had laid down were either scrapped or converted under Hardy's order. A number were converted into corvettes, but some 46-gun frigates continued to be constructed, such as the* Juno *of 1844.*

F

TOP: *The sloops and brigs were also sent to the scrap heap, but again some remained and construction of the type was continued. Typical of this type of vessel were these shown above.*

ABOVE LEFT: *During the 1830s three men were patenting designs for screws. The only man to have any success in presenting his designs to the Admiralty was Francis Pettit Smith. For his work in the field of marine engineering Pettit Smith was later knighted.*

LEFT: *To many officers in the navy the new steam engines were a menace. The pride of the British navy was the sparkling appearance of its warships, which were cleaned and scrubbed from morning till night. Showers of sparks and black soot blew out of the funnels and settled everywhere, thus entailing much extra scrubbing to make the vessels clean.*

ABOVE: *Francis Pettit Smith incorporated his ideas for a screw propeller in the* Archimedes *that was completed in 1839. Although she proved superior in speed and was more economical than the paddle vessel the Admiralty were not fully convinced of the idea, and had many experiments conducted with the* Archimedes.

Steam, however, was by
this time accepted in the
navy. This was
convincingly
demonstrated on August
29, 1842 when Queen
Victoria embarked in
the sailing vessel Royal
George for her first
visit to Scotland. The
Royal George was
towed by two steam
vessels, the Black Eagle
and Shearwater and
escorted by eight other
steam vessels including
the first steam vessels in
the navy, the paddle tug
Monkey, and the
Lightning.

RIGHT: *In the early 1840s the Admiralty carried out a number of experiments to find out the effect of shell fire against the iron plates then being used in the construction of the navy's new warships.   The results were not encouraging, and the First Lord of the Admiralty, the Earl of Auckland—George Eden, had all the iron frigates then under construction scrapped or converted into troopships.*

BELOW: *One of the iron frigates converted for other duties was the troopship* Simoom *shown here some time after her conversion in 1849.*

ABOVE: *One of the earlier iron frigates converted to a troopship was the* Birkenhead *completed in 1845. She was tragically lost off the Cape of Good Hope in South Africa in 1852.*

BELOW: *Following the experiments with the* Archimedes *Lord Dundonald strongly urged the Admiralty to adopt the use of the screw propeller in 1843. There was still scepticism, however, and it was not until 1845 that they finally decided to carry out a test between the screw and paddle. This resulted in the trial of strength between the two sloops* Alecto *and* Rattler.

During the 1840s the navy continued with its survey work, the Rattlesnake, a sixth rate of 1822, charting the Great Barrier Reef off Australia between 1846 and 1850. On board at the time was the world famous scientist Thomas Henry Huxley. In 1853 the Rattlesnake was fitted out and sent on an Arctic expedition.

H. M. Ships *Erebus and Terror*
(Wintered in the Ice in

28 of May 1847 { Lat. 70° 5′ N Long. 98° 23′ W

Having wintered in 1846—7 at Beechey Island
in Lat 74° 43′ 28″ N. Long 91° 39′ 15″ W after having
ascended Wellington Channel to Lat 77° and returned
by the West side of Cornwallis Island

Sir John Franklin commanding the Expedition.
All well

WHOEVER finds this paper is requested to forward it to the Secretary of
the Admiralty, London, *with a note of the time and place at which it was
found:* or, if more convenient, to deliver it for that purpose to the British
Consul at the nearest Port.

QUINCONQUE trouvera ce papier est prié d'y marquer le tems et lieu ou
il l'aura trouvé, et de le faire parvenir au plutot au Secretaire de l'Amirauté
Britannique à Londres.

CUALQUIERA que hallare este Papel, se le suplica de enviarlo al Secretario
del Almirantazgo, en Londrés, con una nota del tiempo y del lugar en
donde se halló.

EEN ieder die dit Papier mogt vinden, wordt hiermede verzogt, om hetzelve, ten spoedigste, te willen zenden aan den Heer Minister van der
Marine der Nederlanden in 's Gravenhage, of wel aan den Secretaris der
Britsche Admiraliteit, te London, en daar by te voegen eene Nota,
inhoudende de tyd en de plaats alwaar dit Papier is gevonden geworden.

FINDEREN af dette Papiir ombedes, naar Leilighed gives, at sende
samme til Admiralitets Secretairen i London, eller nærmeste Embedsmand
i Danmark, Norge, eller Sverrig. Tiden og Stædit hvor dette er fundet
önskes venskabeligt paategnet.

WER diesen Zettel findet, wird hier-durch ersucht denselben an den
Secretair des Admiralitets in London einzusenden, mit gefälliger angabe
an welchen ort und zu welcher zeit er gefunden worden ist.

Party consisting of 2 Officers and 6 Men
left the Ships on Monday 24th May 1847

Gore Lieut
Chas F Des Vœux Mate

LEFT: *On July 26th, 1845 Sir John Franklin had set out on a polar expedition. This was the last that was seen of him for quite some time. During 1848 a number of expeditions were sent to find the explorer, but they all failed. In 1859 yet another expedition set forth and at last met with some success.*

FAR LEFT: *The McClintock expedition found the last record of Sir John Franklin's fatal journey. In a cairn on King William Island Lt. W. R. Hobson found the sheet illustrated here.*

LEFT: *The opening battle of the Crimean War was the action off Sinope, when a Russian Squadron destroyed a Turkish force using the new shell.*

ABOVE: *The first screw propelled warship built for the Admiralty, following the* Alecto–Rattler *experiment, was the* Agamemnon *completed in 1852. During the Crimean war she served in the Black Sea and was finally sold out of service in 1870.*

BELOW: *Following the declaration of war against Russia the Royal Navy at once commenced a blockade of her Black Sea ports. These began on April 22nd, 1854 when Odessa was bombarded. At the point shown in the illustration, the Imperial Mole exploded.*

ABOVE: *One of the casualties of the bombardment of Odessa was the French steamer* Vauban, *which was set on fire by the Russian batteries. A number of vessels from the squadron at once went to her assistance to extinguish the fire. As can be seen from the illustration these were mostly paddle vessels.*

BELOW: *Sebastopol was the next port to be blockaded, and here a very strong allied squadron was assembled, comprised mostly, as can be seen, of sailing ships-of-the-line.*

ABOVE: *The Allied Squadron kept up a very heavy bombardment causing much destruction to the port and the vessels blockaded in it.*

BELOW: *The Baltic squadron of the navy, like the Black Sea fleet, was a very mixed collection of vessels. As the illustration shows there were old wooden sailing ships-of-the-line, wooden screw ships-of-the-line, iron paddle steamers and many others.*

Later in the war, on October 17th, 1854, the flagship of the Black Sea fleet, the Agamemnon, under Admiral Sir Edward Lyons, carried out a bombardment of Fort Constantine in the Black Sea.

RIGHT: *The Baltic Fleet had originally been under command of Admiral Sir Charles Napier, but in 1855 he was replaced by Vice-Admiral Sir J. W. Dundas, GCB, shown here. Admiral Dundas had formerly been in command of the Black Sea Fleet.*

BELOW: *Under Admiral Dundas a survey was carried out of the Baltic port of Sveaborg. The port had previously been blockaded, but without much success. In the* Merlin, *Admiral Dundas sailed right up to the port, and as shown, the Russians were not slow to attack him, floating their new mines against his little ship.*

ABOVE: *Following the surveying of Sveaborg, the Baltic squadron carried out a close bombardment of the port.*

BELOW: *On board his flagship, the* Wellington, *Admiral Dundas was well entertained by the Baltic squadron on the conclusion of the successful bombardment of Sveaborg.*

In the Baltic the winter was severe, forcing the British squadron to leave the area and winter at home. In the Black Sea the fleet continued the blockade, but the weather in that area was also severe as shown in the illustration. The picture shows the Royal Albert blockading Sevastopol during a snow storm.

Further down the Black Sea an expedition was landed to take the peninsula of Kertch. The illustration shows the troops disembarking with the St. Paul's battery blowing up in the background.

G

ABOVE: *While the Crimean War was in progress the Admiralty continued to fit out Polar expeditions. Two of these expeditions were under command of Commander Edward Augustus Inglefield, in the yacht* Isabel. *The picture shows the* Isabel *sailing through Smith Sound in the Arctic. This was the first time that a ship had entered the Sound, and from it Commander Inglefield discovered the Polar Sea at midnight on August 26th, 1852.*

RIGHT: *Towards the end of the Crimean War the Admiralty appointed a committee under Rear-Admiral the Hon. Henry John Rous to draw up designs for a standard uniform for the ordinary seaman. Before coming to a final decision Admiral Rous put the propositions before the Admirals commanding the bases at Portsmouth and Plymouth.*

LEFT: *The main point of discord had been the rows of white tape round the collar, which in January 1857 were standardised to three rows. An earlier variation shown left depicts a sailor with two rows.*

BELOW LEFT: *William George Armstrong formed the first modern British armament firm at Elswick, from where in 1855 he produced a new type of gun designed to fire shells not cannon balls. Originally trained as a solicitor, Armstrong became an engineer at 37, and apart from designing guns was also responsible for construction of a hydraulic crane.*

BELOW: *Another engineer who also spent much time experimenting with gun designs, was Joseph Whitworth of Manchester. Later the firms of the two engineers combined to form the engineering firm of Armstrong-Whitworth.*

ABOVE: *The ultimate development of the "wooden walls" was the three-decker line of battle ship—the* Victoria. *This wooden screwed vessel was the last of her type to leave harbour as a sea-going ship.*

BELOW: *Even on the new wooden screw ships-of-the-line conditions were no different from those at the turn of the century. In high seas and raging gales life on board was practically intolerable. The picture depicts the screw vessel* Conqueror, *completed in 1855.*

ABOVE: *Rear-Admiral Sir Michael Seymour was Commander-in-Chief of the China Station when the Second China War broke out, was in charge of the force which captured Canton on October 25th, 1856 and was in command at the destruction of the Taku Forts on August 20th, 1858.*

LEFT: *When trouble broke out in China in April 1859 the new Commander-in-Chief of the China Station was Rear-Admiral Sir James Hope. He at once gathered together a squadron to force the Peiho river. Having subdued the Peiho Forts at the mouth of the river, he too had to attack the Taku Forts, which had again been taken over by rebels.*

LEFT: *In 1857 the surveyor of the navy, Mr. Baldwin Wake-Walker, designed a new class of large frigates. In size they were almost the same as a number of two and three decker ships-of-the-line then in service. One of these vessels was the* Ariadne *of 4400 tons completed in 1859. As such these frigates formed the link between ships like the* Victoria *and the new broadside ironclad* Warrior, *just about to be laid down.*

BELOW: *In reply to the French ironclads under construction, about which the Admiralty had received information, two new vessels were laid down in British yards. Taking as their background the design of the* Ariadne *type of frigates these two vessels were planned with an iron belt along their waterline. Laid down in May 1859 the first of the new ironclads was named the* Warrior.

ABOVE: *The first ironclad to be completed in the world was the French* La Gloire. *She was not, however, as powerful as the British* Warrior, *at that time under construction.*

RIGHT: *The man responsible for the design of Britain's first ironclad was John Scott Russell who was born in 1808.*

LEFT: *After the attack in October 1856 Admiral Seymour was forced to abandon Canton, due to lack of support forces. To assist him, a stronger force was sent out from England in June 1857. The flotilla was mainly composed of the ubiquitous gunboats, some of which stopped at Madeira as shown on their way out to China.*

BELOW LEFT: *So that the force of ironclads could be rapidly increased, without having to wait for new construction, it was decided to convert three wooden vessels into ironclads. One of these was the* Favourite *shown in 1869.*

BELOW: *During the 1860s there was further trouble from pirates in the China Sea. The gunboats of the Royal Navy were continually in action protecting merchantmen. Occasionally forays were made to seek out the pirates in their lairs. The action shown took place in June 1867 between the* Cormorant *and pirates from Formosa.*

RIGHT: *During all these troubles in the Far East the Commander-in-Chief of the station was Rear-Admiral Augustus Kuper.   He later rose to the rank of Vice-Admiral and was awarded the CB for his services.*

BELOW: *The direct descendants of the ironclad* Warrior *were the two smaller vessels* Defence *and* Resistance.   *The photograph shows the* Defence *as completed, carrying eight 7in BLR guns.   She was re-armed in 1867 with two 8in and fourteen 7in MLR guns.*

Off the East African coasts the slave-trade still lingered on, with the Arabs trading heavily in slaves. This continued on and off right up to the 1870s. Again, gunboats were the main vessels used in the task of intercepting and capturing the slavers. One such incident is shown here where the gunboat Teazer captured the slaver Abbot Devereux in 1857.

ABOVE: *As the ironclad programme was getting under way the navy was expanding its bases throughout the world. One of the oldest of these foreign bases was the bastion of Gibraltar. In the illustration, taken in 1864, two of the newest ironclads of the time can be seen. In front is the* Resistance, *while behind is the converted wooden ship* Royal Oak.

OPPOSITE, TOP: *The* Hector *and* Valiant *followed the* Defence *and* Resistance, *and were really modifications of the* Defence. *The* Hector *was the first to be completed, in 1864, and was armed with four 7in BLR guns. The* Valiant *was not completed until 1868, when she reverted to muzzle-loading armament. The illustration shows the* Hector *as completed in 1864.*

OPPOSITE, CENTRE: *The* Achilles, *shown here in 1866, was originally to have been similar to the* Warrior, *but she was redesigned to enable her to have an armour belt the full length of her waterline.*

OPPOSITE, FOOT: *The* Agincourt, Minotaur *and* Northumberland *had the distinction of being the longest, single screw warships ever built, being 400 feet long, and were designed as the most heavily armed vessels then afloat. They carried four 9in MLR, twenty-four 7in MLR and eight 24-pdr guns. The illustration shows the* Agincourt *in 1868.*

ABOVE: *The above illustration shows the after part of the* Minotaur *just after completion in 1868. In the left foreground is a 7in MLR gun. The* Minotaur *was notable for being the first ship in the fleet to be fitted with a searchlight.*

BELOW: *In an effort to commission as many ironclads as possible, the Admiralty converted a number of wooden ships-of-the-line. The* Royal Oak *was one of these, and she is shown above after being re-armed in 1867.*

ABOVE: *The dockyards had always kept large stocks of timber to construct the wooden walls, but the coming of the ironclad meant that these stocks would no longer be needed. In an effort to clear the timber three wooden ironclads were ordered, one of these being the* Lord Warden *shown above in 1867.*

BELOW: *The gunboats of the navy had more than shown their worth during the Crimean War. Out of these grew an idea to construct large armoured gunboats, using the new ironclad principles, and three of the new type of vessel were ordered. The* Waterwitch *shown here in 1867, was fitted with a new type of engine which unfortunately proved unsatisfactory.*

LEFT: *One of the great inventors of the decade was Captain Cowper Phipps Coles. Following up ideas he had formulated during the Crimean War, Captain Coles perfected a turret system for carrying guns in an armoured enclosure, but still giving them freedom of movement. His plans were put to the test in a number of experimental ships, his final effort being to design and supervise the construction of the* Captain, *in which he unfortunately lost his life in 1870.*

The first ship to be fitted with one of Captain Coles' turrets was the Royal Sovereign. *She was an old wooden three-decker, but had her top two decks removed and four turrets fitted. In addition to her turrets the* Royal Sovereign *was given an armour belt which extended the length of her waterline.*

LEFT: *The Chief Constructor of the navy at the time Captain Coles was developing his turret, was Edward Reed. Born at Sheerness in September 1830 Reed served a four-year apprenticeship at the dockyard, before being selected to go to the school of mathematics and Naval Construction at Portsmouth. He left when the school was abolished in 1852, becoming editor of the* Mechanics Magazine *which he developed as a naval journal. He later rejoined the constructors department and became Chief Constructor, also serving on the Institute of Naval Architects. He was responsible for the many varying ironclad designs developed during the era. The photograph was taken about two years after he became Chief Constructor.*

BELOW: *Almost at the same time as conversion work started on the* Royal Sovereign *a new ship was laid down, especially designed to carry four of Coles' turrets. This ship was the* Prince Albert *shown below.*

H

ABOVE: *Reed developed and introduced the "bracket-frame" system of construction during his term of office. This method was first used in the* Bellerophon *shown above in 1885 after being re-rigged as a barque, and re-armed with ten 8in BLR guns.*

BELOW: *The* Bellerophon *was followed by the* Hercules, *virtually a sister ship to the* Bellerophon. *The* Hercules *was, however, larger, and carried new 10in MLR guns as opposed to the 9in MLR of the* Bellerophon. *The photograph shows her during her first commission in 1868. In 1872 she rammed the* Northumberland *during a gale and as a result of the collision her bottom was torn open and the wing compartments flooded.*

In June 1866 a number of tests were carried out to see how Captain Coles' turret would stand up to heavy gunfire. To carry out the trials the Royal Sovereign was used as a target at which the Bellerophon fired three rounds of 9in shell at a range of 200 yards. The hits were recorded on the front, back and glacis of the turret, failing to cause any damage to the turning mechanism of the turret. The two top pictures show the effect of the first shot on the front of the turret from outside (left) and inside (right). The lower pictures show the dislocation of the plates at the back of the turret on the second shot (left), and of the third shot which glanced on the glacis (right).

EFFECTS OF FIRST SHOT—INTERIOR OF TURRET.

EFFECTS OF THIRD SHOT.

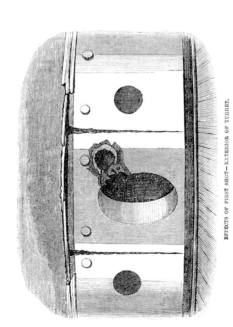

EFFECTS OF FIRST SHOT—EXTERIOR OF TURRET.

EFFECTS OF SECOND SHOT

TOP: *The* Penelope *was officially rated as an armoured corvette. She was designed with an exceptionally shallow draught and completed with two screws, which could be raised, and two rudders. With a shallow draught and raised screws, the* Penelope *was ideal for shallow coastal duties.*

ABOVE: *One firm of shipbuilders gained a great deal of experience constructing turret ships. Lairds of Birkenhead had built turret vessels, not only for the Royal Navy, but also for foreign powers. Two such vessels were the* Scorpion *and* Wivern *originally ordered for the Confederate Navy, but requisitioned for the Royal Navy. In the picture the hinged sides amidships are seen lowered, unmasking the turrets.*

TOP: *The first sea-going ship to be armed with turret guns was the* Monarch *completed in 1869. The photograph shows the 12in gunned vessel about 1875.*

ABOVE: *Captain Coles' final design was the* Captain. *This ship was also built by Lairds, under supervision by Captain Coles. Although the plans were passed, many misgivings were had both by the Admiralty and the Chief Constructor Edward Reed as to the advisability of constructing the ship. Such was the public support for Captain Coles, both in the press and Parliament, that he was given permission to go ahead and construct the vessel. The misgivings were confirmed when the vessel capsized in a gale in 1870. The illustration shows the* Captain *during completion.*

LEFT: *During the 1860s the conditions of service for the men vastly improved. With the great technological advances being made many new branches of seamanship were formed, and the way for promotion greatly eased. The illustration shows a typical Victorian sailor in 1860.*

ABOVE: *During the 1860s the navy was engaged in a number of minor operations throughout the world. One of the most turbulent areas was along the African coast. One of these minor wars was the Ashanti war, and the illustration shows the troops re-embarking at Cape Coast Castle on September 24th, 1864 at the conclusion of the operation. In all these minor conflicts the navy was always responsible for transporting the troops, and often assisted them with naval landing parties.*

ABOVE LEFT: *In September 1870 the* Captain *capsized in a gale. Already much feeling had been aroused in the Admiralty over the construction of the vessel, and her loss gave rise to even greater friction in certain quarters. One of those most upset by the sinking of the* Captain *was the First Lord Hugh Childers. He had lost his only son when the* Captain *went down, and became so bitter over the affair that he placed the whole blame for the loss on the Constructors department, forcing the Controller, Sir Spencer Robinson to resign.*

ABOVE: *The Controller was not the only man to resign his post over the* Captain *affair. Already Reed had resigned following violent disagreements with Captain Coles concerning the construction of the vessel. His position as Chief Constructor was taken by his brother-in-law, Nathaniel Barnaby. Barnaby held rather different views from Reed on the concept of the ironclad. While in the Constructors department Barnaby carried out a number of theoretical calculations on stability and had produced figures that showed that the* Captain *might capsize before she was ever completed. The illustration shows Barnaby in later years after having been knighted and awarded the KCB for his work in the engineering field.*

ABOVE: *The final climax of the* Captain *affair was the resignation of the First Lord of the Admiralty, Hugh Childers. All the worry and strife caused by the incident gave rise to a serious illness, which forced him to resign his post. His place was taken by G. J. Goschen (above) who remained at the Admiralty for three years, during which time he formed the Naval Volunteers.*

ABOVE: *The next ironclads to be completed were those of the* Audacious *class. The class was designed by Reed and had far better accommodation for the crew than most ships of the time. The illustration shows the* Audacious.

BELOW: *The* Triumph *was almost identical to the* Audacious *class, differing only in minor details. Together with her sister ship* Swiftsure *she underwent an Admiralty experiment regarding the feasibility of reintroducing copper-sheathing to the hulls of naval vessels. The hulls of the two vessels were completely different from those of the* Audacious, *and they further differed in having a full ship rig. The photograph is of the* Triumph *just after completion. After their first commission these two ships were given a barque rig i.e. no square sails carried on the after mast (mizzen mast).*

ABOVE: *The* Sultan, *completed in 1871, was virtually an improved type of* Hercules *designed by Reed. Like a number of other ships in the fleet originally completed with a full rig, the* Sultan *was reduced to a barque rig after four years of service. The illustration shows the vessel with a barque rig about 1877.*

LEFT: *One of the more peculiar designs developed during the 1870s was that for the breastwork monitor* Glatton. *She had an extremely low freeboard on which she carried two 12in MLR in a single turret.*

ABOVE: *Another strange vessel with a distinct function was the ram vessel* Hotspur. *She was completed in 1871 and is shown on service in the Sea of Marmora during the Russo-Turkish war of 1877.*

BELOW: *The* Hotspur *was followed by another ram, the* Rupert. *Unlike the* Hotspur, *whose gun was mounted behind a fixed embrasure, the* Rupert *carried her two 10in MLR guns in a turret. She served with the* Hotspur *during the Russo-Turkish war and is shown in a Mediterranean port sometime during that period.*

ABOVE: *During the war scare of 1870 plans were laid down for four coast defence ships. The vessels were quickly launched, but the scare died and work slowed down. The Hydra shown above was not completed until 1876.*

BELOW: *The* Devastation *was the first turret ship in the navy to be completed without any sailing masts and yet be designed for sailing with the battle fleet. The illustration shows the* Devastation *in 1887. Her sister ship, the* Thunderer, *suffered a severe explosion with her muzzle-loading guns in 1879, when eleven men were killed and thirty injured. This accident to some extent helped hasten the reintroduction of the breech-loading gun.*

A planned sister ship of the Devastation, *was the* Fury. *After the reports of the Special Committee on Designs were received, however, she was completely replanned and emerged as the* Dreadnought. *The illustration shows the vessel at Malta, one of the bases developed for the navy in the Mediterranean. She was so designed that when joining action the topmast would be struck, the railings lowered on the deck, boats trailed astern as in the old days, and the bulwarks in the bows dropped.*

OPPOSITE, TOP: *In the photograph of Malta taken sometime between 1873 and 1874, many of the differing types of vessel forming the battle fleet can be seen. From left to right they are: the* Thunderer (Invincible *behind*), Alexandra (Rupert *behind*) *and the* Monarch.

OPPOSITE, LEFT: *Yet another ram vessel designed during the 1870s was the* Polyphemus. *She had originally been designed for ramming but during construction had five submerged torpedo tubes fitted as well as the ram bow.*

ABOVE: *In 1873 the Shah of Persia visited England and in the summer of that year was aboard the Royal Yacht* Victoria and Albert *when the naval review was held at Spithead. In honour of his visit the large unarmoured frigate* Blonde *then under construction was renamed* Shah.

*The torpedo itself was an invention of a
Mr. Whitehead working at Fiume. The
first torpedo designed was 14in in diameter
and pointed at both ends. It weighed 300lb
and had a speed of 6 knots. The explosive
charge in the nose weighed 18lb. The
illustration shows a 16in torpedo of 1870
which had a charge of 76lb of guncotton
and with a speed of 8 knots it had a range
of 400 yards.*

*In 1872 the wooden steam corvette
Challenger set sail on a scientific expedition
to the Atlantic, Pacific and Antarctic seas.
She was away for 3½ years and covered
nearly 70,000 miles. The photograph above
shows her at an anchorage somewhere on her
voyage.*

On board the Challenger *was Captain William J. J. Spry.*

In charge of the research work on the Challenger *expedition was Professor Wyville Thompson. In the photograph he is shown seated, with Dr. Suhm and an assistant beside him on St. Thomas Island in the West Indies.*

I

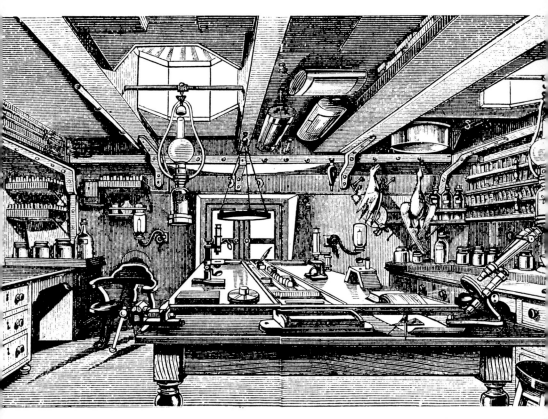

The scientists' room on board the Challenger *was fitted out with all the most modern equipment then available for their research.*

ABOVE: *The* Alexandra (*ex*-Superb), *completed in 1877, proved to be the fastest battleship afloat at that time. There were one or two interesting points about the Alexandra, perhaps the most notable being that she was one of the last broadside ironclads with her main armament sited below decks. Another interesting feature of the armament was that her broadside was considerably reduced in power and the guns so sited that ahead fire was greatly increased.*

BELOW: *While the Alexandra was under construction a new vessel was laid down at Chatham. This vessel, the* Temeraire, *was designed to carry her guns in a new type of mounting. Two new 25 ton 11in guns were to be carried fore and aft on a new type of carriage, emplaced in a barbette. One of the 11in guns is shown in the firing position. To load the gun it was hydraulically lowered below the sides of the barbette. The* Temeraire *was the first barbette ship in the Royal Navy and was the largest brig rigged ship constructed for the service.*

ABOVE: *During the 1870s the ram became a powerful concept in the minds of a number of naval officers, and its possible value was proved in a tragic accident on September 1st, 1875. While carrying out manoeuvres in fog, off the coast of Ireland, the* Iron Duke *rammed the* Vanguard *amidships. Within a short space of time the* Vanguard *had sunk, fortunately without loss of life.*

BELOW: *The last wooden warships constructed for the Royal Navy were the* Amethyst *class corvettes, carrying fourteen 64-pdrs. The* Amethyst *shown here in 1874 was completed in 1873.*

ABOVE: *Another vessel typical of her type was the sloop* Albatross. *Practically all the sloops constructed during the 1870s were similar to the* Albatross, *which was completed in 1873. The picture shows the vessel in harbour in 1874.*

BELOW: *An action involving vessels of the Royal Navy that occurred on May 29th, 1877 was notable for the fact that for the first time a Whitehead torpedo was used in action. Involved in the action were the unarmoured frigate* Shah *and the corvette* Amethyst. *They had been sent to exact retribution from the Peruvian* Huascar *that had been seized by rebels during an attempted* coup. *The* Huascar *was heavily damaged during the action and sailed away during the night to surrender to the Peruvian Government forces.*

ABOVE: *The* Shah *carried an exceptionally heavy armament for a frigate. It comprised two 9in MLR, eight 7in MLR and eight 64-pdrs. The photograph shows the vessel in 1875.*

BELOW: *Following the excellent principles developed in the* Inflexible *design, the Admiralty ordered two smaller versions of this design which proved to be the most unsatisfactory ships ever completed for service. The Ajax and Agamemnon were the last battleships to carry MLR guns. The design called for a draught shallow enough to enable the vessels to operate in the Baltic or Black Sea. With the advent of the torpedo means of combating torpedo carrying craft was necessary and these two vessels were the first to be fitted with a secondary armament (two 6in BLR guns) in addition to their anti-torpedo nets. The illustration shows the* Ajax.

ABOVE: *The torpedo was now a weapon to be reckoned with, and the school set up by Captain Fisher to instruct men in the use of the torpedo was well established in the navy. The photograph shows such a torpedo class in 1876.*

LEFT: *By the end of the 1870s many great advances had been made in the field of marine engineering. The photograph shows four men who were responsible for many innovations in the navy. They are (left to right) John Penn (1805–1878) who developed marine engines, Joseph Whitworth (1803–1887) who made a number of improvements to guns, Robert Napier (1791–1876) who also developed steam engines and Sir William Fairbairn (1789–1874).*

On March 24th, 1878 the sixth rate frigate Eurydice, *built in 1843, foundered off the Isle of Wight. Following the foundering attempts were made in April 1878 to raise the vessel. The upper picture shows the position of the capsized vessel with her topmasts just above water. The lower illustration shows vessels engaged in the salvage operations. A chain has just been placed under the hull of the wrecked vessel.*

In 1875 another Arctic expedition set forth,
under Sir George Nares in the Alert. So
keen were the sailors for these expeditions
that a whole ship's company of 800
volunteered for this expedition. The party
did not reach the Pole, but got the nearest
that man had then been. As winter
descended the men had to race to find a
cove to shelter in before the ice cut them off.
They dragged the boat stern first into the
cove where they were at once sealed in by
the ice as shown above. The temperature
was 105 degrees below freezing point.

The ice completely sealed the entrance to the cove, and as it passed the rocks, great lumps of ice weighing over 30,000 tons broke off and piled up in blocks 300 feet broad and 50 feet high.

ABOVE: *While wintering in the cove the men made great friends with some Eskimos shown above.*

OPPOSITE, TOP: *During the Russo-Turkish war scare of 1877 a number of vessels under construction in Great Britain for those countries were taken over by the Royal Navy. One of these was the Turkish* Peik-i-Sheref, *which had been designed in Constantinople as an armour-plated ram. On commissioning for the navy she was renamed* Belleisle *and reclassed as a coast defence ship.*

OPPOSITE, RIGHT: *With the success of the torpedo assured the navy constructed the torpedo boat* Lightning *in 1877. At the time two other torpedo boats were under construction for Russia. These were taken over in 1877 and were followed by a number of other similar craft. The photograph right taken in 1878 shows a number of torpedo craft. On the larger boat note the torpedo tube in the bows and the Whitehead torpedo on a trolley abreast the funnel.*

ABOVE: *In 1878 the* Comus, *the first of a class of six vessels, entered the navy and became the first vessel completely built of steel to fly the white ensign. Officially classed as a corvette, she was later rerated as a protected cruiser. The illustration above shows the* Conquest, *a sister ship of the* Comus, *chasing an Arab slave dhow in 1892.*

OPPOSITE, TOP: *Most of the Arab slave dhows operated out of Zanzibar, and the navy kept a permanent squadron in the area to intercept the traffic. This was a dangerous task requiring courage and enterprise, as the officers in charge of the operations were usually only junior lieutenants.*

OPPOSITE, RIGHT: *The* Inflexible, *completed in 1881, was the first British capital ship to carry her guns en echelon. At the time the 16in guns were the heaviest afloat.*

W. H. OVEREND.

*During the 1870s unrest continued off the
West African coast as well as the East
Coast. In order to subdue the Africans,
Commodore Sir William Hewett, VC, in
the* Active, *took a force up the River Niger.
The illustration shows him offering presents
to Tribal Chiefs on board the* Encounter
at Bonny Town in June 1875.